Michael P
POCKET G
BAIT AN

D1646446

Michael Prichard started writing in the hard school of Fleet Street, and having acquired the skills of the journalist he left for quieter waters. As a fishing tackle adviser, he travels far and wide in the pursuit of good tackle design. He has directed a number of angling films, and broadcasts regularly on radio and TV.

With a life-long fascination with fishing in all its forms, Mike has sought every species of interest to the sportfisherman and succeeded in taking many fine specimens from freshwater and saltwater. His prowess with the camera (he is an Associate of the Royal Photographic Society) enables him to publish first-class evidence of his catches. In 1978 and 1979 Mike captained England at International Sea Fishing festivals in Connemara and Youghal, Eire, and in both years his team beat strong opposition from the rest of the British and Continental teams. For many years he also organized the popular Guinness sea angling contests in Dingle, Eire.

A desire to pass on his wide knowledge of the sport has led to the encouragement and instruction of young anglers in many areas of Britain. Among the author's books are his *Pocket Guide to Saltwater Fishing*, *Pocket Guide to Freshwater Fishing* (the companions to this book), the best-selling *Encyclopedia of Fishing in Britain and Ireland* and *Fishing for Beginners*, all published by Collins. He contributes regularly to *Sea Angler* and *Rod and Gun* magazines.

COMPANION BOOKS

Michael Prichard's Pocket Guide to Saltwater Fishing
Michael Prichard's Pocket Guide to Freshwater Fishing

Michael Prichard's
POCKET GUIDE TO
BAIT
AND LURES

Collins

Published by William Collins Sons & Co. Ltd.
London and Glasgow.
© Michael Prichard 1983
First published 1983

Printed and bound in Great Britain by
William Collins Sons & Co. Ltd.

ISBN 0 00 411697 6

CONTENTS

INTRODUCTION

Fishing is all about luring a wild animal into taking a bait that may, or may not, be something that it regards as food. Without doubt the angler's bait is the most important part of his tackle, without a suitable hookbait the best rods and most expensive reels would be useless. On the other hand a relatively simple and inexpensive tackle set-up with a first-class bait will surely catch fish—if there are any in the vicinity.

There are a number of natural baits that fish are conditioned to find in the course of their daily lives; grubs will fall from bankside vegetation and many creatures that live in water have a larval stage that fish feed on. Land drains constantly carry worms from the surrounding earth, particularly after heavy rainfall has brought flood conditions to the rivers and streams.

Anglers use a variety of baits not normally found in the countryside. These baits, such as bread, succeed because we have progressively introduced this form of food to fish and the shoals have learned. Some lures, those made of metal, plastic and feather, rely on movement to attract. They simulate the movements of small fish, animals and insects that form part of the diet of all predators. The key to a successful bait lies in presenting a hook offering in such a way as to induce the fish into taking it as food, or arousing the predatory instinct that is latent within most water-living creatures.

When fishing in saltwater we tend to use only those baits that are found in the wild. Sea fish are not captive within any established area of water so they rarely stay long enough to be conditioned to anglers' offerings. And since most hooked fish are eaten by the fisherman, little opportunity exists for any form of acquired behaviour. Artificial lures play an important role in sea angling, largely because there are seasons when livebait is difficult to gather. In saltwater, lure action seems to be more important than a perfect representation of something that the fish would recognise as food. This need for vibration and movement allows all manner of materials to be pressed into service in the construction of lures as sea fishing baits.

This Pocket Guide is concerned with the multitude of fishing baits: how to gather, preserve and present them. The subject is a fascinating one that extends a vital aspect of the sport of angling. From merely buying commercially produced hook baits the angler can enter the realm of becoming a countrywise collector or avid beachcomber.

Michael Prichard, ARPS

The first essential to becoming a successful sportfisherman: ensure that your bait is of top quality and is perfectly presented.

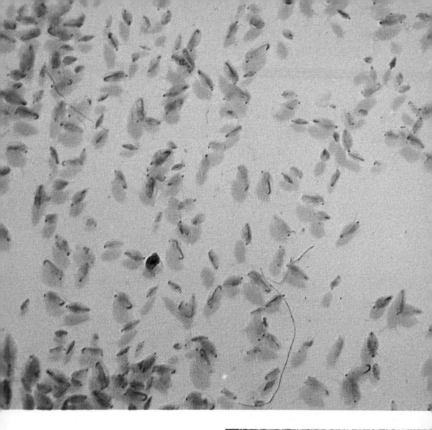

Above *Daphnia, other small crustaceans and tiny snails form much of the natural food of fish of all sizes and species.* Right *Night-time worm gathering by torchlight. The worms have to be grasped firmly to prevent their retreating back down the hole. However, they have no bony structure and therefore fracture easily when handled roughly by being yanked from their burrow.*

FISHING WITH WORMS

If we consider the sport of angling throughout the ages, one bait stands alone. No matter where fishing was done, or how it was undertaken, the earthworm seems to have been the angler's lure. The lowly worm was the natural fish catcher long before fishermen became sophisticated in their choice of hookbaits.

Of the kinds of worm available to the freshwater angler the lobworm is the most important. Found in the open fields, suburban gardens and on tiny lawns of city dwellers, the lobworm is an ever-present cornerstone of our ecology. Lobworms do more work in improving the quality of soil than the plough. And during periods of heavy rainfall, these worms are often washed from the land mass into streams and rivers. Fish have therefore become used to eating them, so although the worms wouldn't naturally form part of their everyday diet they are eagerly taken.

There is some truth in the belief that worms are regarded, by anglers, as catchers of big fish. Small fish cannot swallow a whole lobworm as easily as they can the minute food particles found in rivers and lakes. Fish are attracted by the movement of a lobworm bait and the smell that is given off by the juices that exude from the worm. Their frantic feeding activity is often the signal for larger fish to move into the swim.

Finding a sufficient number of lobworms for a fishing trip is a relatively easy task. The casts on a lawn are evidence of their presence. These casts look like coils of fine earth. Each whorl is thrown up at the top of the worm's tunnel and are the end product of the creature's feeding activity. Having established that there are worms to be had from a lawn, the problem is how and when to gather them. Since lobworms are creatures active at night it is pointless to expect the worm to emerge during daylight hours.

Without doubt the best worm-gathering time is on a dark night, humid after a freshening shower of rain. Since it is dark, a torch is necessary to see the worms that have come up to lie on the surface. A bright beam is not needed, it will only make the lobs dive back down into their holes. You need just enough light to enable you to see where the worms are. Tread carefully and softly, for worms can detect vibrations that footsteps make over long distances.

Ideally you should have both hands free to capture worms. This means you need a companion to hold the torch, or it must be attached on your person. I'm lucky in being a sea angler as well, so I have a shore fisher's light which is attached to my hat, with the battery box on a fixture on my belt. This illumination gives me both hands free and a light that accurately follows every turn of the head. Divide the worm catching area into sections. Don't go walking haphazardly around, it will disturb worms outside the lamplit area. Walk carefully forward until you see a worm; stop and size up how the worm is lying. The head will be out on the grass *but* the tail will be still in the hole and *that* is the clue to losing the worm. Too much vibration or light and the worm will retract its head and body into the tunnel like lightning. You can prevent its escape by grasping the worm firmly behind its head and continuing to hold it while the worm wriggles and thrashes. But this violent movement helps in its capture. Its wriggling often causes the worm's tail to leave the hole. As the worm loses purchase and relaxes it can be pulled gently away from the hole.

Handling worms can be a slippery, messy business. I use a pair of thin, soft gloves when bait gathering. The texture of the gloves helps me to grasp the animal and prevent it slipping through my fingers without having to apply too much pressure. Worms are easily injured and broken lobs quickly lose their body fluids and thereby their angling attractiveness.

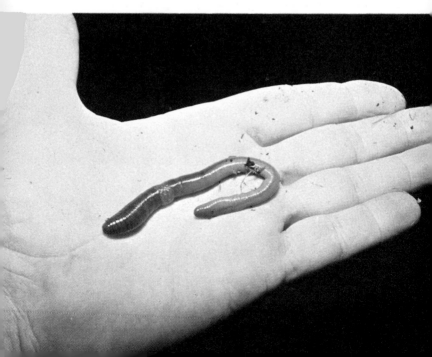

The dry periods of spring and summer are times when lobworms cannot be collected. We resort then to digging for them, but they may be down really deep. At these times we have to bring the worms closer to the surface by careful watering of the ground. It is not necessary to create a flood but just enough moisture to get the worms on an upward migration. Some people advise using water to which is added washing up liquid. I don't use this method because I value my lawn but I know that it does force worms up on to the grass. If you want to use this method, wash them well before putting them on the hook to remove all traces of the detergent. Fish are easily put off by tainted baits.

Hooking a lobworm

All too often the lobworm is hooked without thought to its ability to attract fish. The angler, smitten with the fact that the worm must not get off the hook, pierces it too many times by the point. But this over-enthusiastic hooking results in the quick death of the worm—and a dead

Left The earliest fishermen knew that the lobworm is a fine bait, but it must be hooked correctly to be effective by wriggling in an attractive manner. Below Two methods of mounting the lobworm: A (below right), the single hook, and B (left), the two-hook Pennell rig (see page 12).

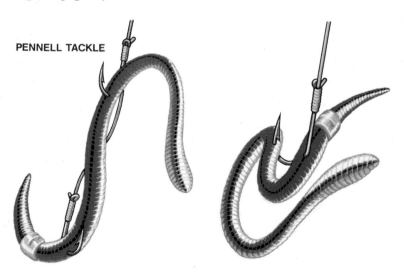

PENNELL TACKLE

worm *does not* make an attractive bait. The idea is to present the worm in such a way that it looks perfectly natural and retains the ability to wriggle. Fish are encouraged to feed by the way in which the bait moves—if we prevent that, the whole baiting set-up is ruined.

The lobworm can measure any size from a couple of inches to nearly a foot long. So it follows that hook size is vitally important. A small hook will tear out from a big worm, whereas too large a hook would quickly kill a small lob. You must balance the bait to the iron size carefully. The following table gives some idea of relative hook sizes:

2–3 in (50–75 mm) worms	No. 14–16 hook size
4–6 in (100–150 mm) worms	No. 10–12 hook size
Large worms	No. 8 hook size at least

You will notice that the hook size has not been related to fish species. This is simply because fishing cannot be selective by bait size or hook size. A particular bait will attract certain fish but it cannot determine the size of fish that arrives!

I am convinced that Method A gives the best presentation pattern for a medium sized lobworm. The hook is passed twice through the worm at the positions shown. Although securely held the worm is allowed to move naturally, both head and tail, in a lively fashion. Tentative bites by a cautious fish often pull a worm off the hook when pierced once. The double-hooked principle gives added security in that a plucking bite may still mean that the worm remains on.

I use Method B when fishing a lobworm to zander and big perch. Both species are renowned for their delicate feeding behaviour and ability to tweak the worm from a paternostered rig. Setting the lobworm up on the two-hook Pennell tackle stops the fish from biting off the tail of the worm, leaving you the body on the hook. Use the system for a really large worm that is fished in mid-water.

Small lobworms, intended for smaller sized fish, can be fished in pieces. The tail of a lob is especially attractive to roach. Nip off about an inch of worm and thread it onto the hook, hiding most of the bend and shank within the scrap of worm. This baiting style can be adapted into a cocktail bait by the addition of a maggot covering the hook point and barb. The fish will be attracted both by the lively antics of the grub and the powerful smell of the worm's body contents.

The smallest worms can be fished bunched onto a medium size hook, No. 12–14. Simply nick the worms once and let them hang on the bend of the iron. Big fish can take the bunch easily, while their smaller brethren may steal the odd worm but leave enough to come back for

The tail of a lobworm makes a fine roach and bream bait, especially when enlivened by the addition of a wriggling maggot on the hook.

MAGGOT/WORM COCKTAIL

more. Any fear they might have of the hookbait is minimised by the ease in which they took the preliminary mouthful.

Keeping lobworms

We do not always have time to gather worms at a moment's notice and there are many occasions when a worm-collecting foray is not possible before a fishing trip. What is needed therefore is a storage system. Worms are a living commodity that cannot be stored outside their environment. The answer is to create a worm farm. There are two ways to do this: captive farming, or an ideal, free, habitat from which the worms will not want to escape.

The captive wormery

The easiest and cleanest worm farm can be made from a strong plastic sack similar to those in which plants such as tomatoes are grown. The sack, preferably a black one if the wormery has to be placed in a position subjected to strong daylight, is filled with carefully selected materials that will ensure drainage, warmth and food for the inhabitants. Make a number of holes in the bottom of the sack so that excess water can run away. Cover the holes with a wad of chopped newspaper that will assist drainage while retaining some moisture in the drier periods of the year. Fill the sack at least half full with a mixture of well-rotted compost and garden loam. Over this a layer of manure is added. Pig manure is the best food substance, providing the family will stand for it! The sack system does cut down on unpleasant smells but some odour is inevitable.

To this basic wormery add as a food source a constant supply of

Redworms and brandlings can be bred with little effort, easily and at low cost. The main essentials are a healthy environment and regular feeding with the correct nutrition. Below The captive wormery, which can be sited in almost any garden. Below right The open worm farm needs special positioning to be successful.

THE CAPTIVE WORMERY

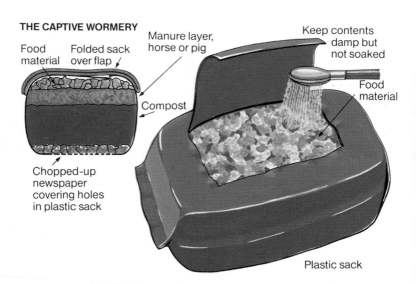

Food material

Folded sack over flap

Manure layer, horse or pig

Compost

Chopped-up newspaper covering holes in plastic sack

Keep contents damp but not soaked

Food material

Plastic sack

vegetable scraps, potato peelings, tea leaves, root vegetable tops and a small amount of grass cuttings. The farm is started off by introducing a number of mature worms which should be left to breed in peace. Moisture must be added at frequent intervals, applied with a watering can. After closing the top flap, a thick, folded hessian sack must be used as a covering through which both air and light rain can penetrate. This is vitally important as the worms need both if they are to convert the food into a new generation of hookbaits. Anglers who require a constant supply of worms might well invest in two wormeries, one for breeding purposes and the other in which to keep the mature hookbaits that are ready for fishing use.

The open wormery

Site selection is vital for the open worm farm. Begin by selecting a shaded, slightly damp part of your garden. Direct sunlight is unnecessary. Make a simple wooden box, about 18 in (46 cm) high, forming only the sides, as a top and bottom are not needed. Place the box on a sheet of thick plastic that has been pierced with a garden fork. This will keep the worms captive yet allow proper drainage. An inch-deep (2.5 cm) layer of fine stones is then laid over the plastic sheet to ensure that sudden rainstorms will not waterlog the farm.

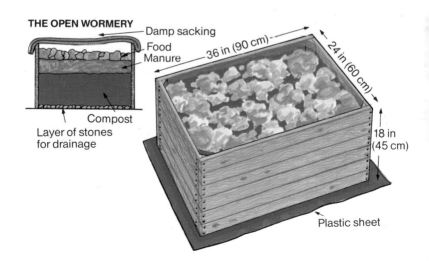

THE OPEN WORMERY
Damp sacking
Food
Manure
36 in (90 cm)
24 in (60 cm)
Compost
Layer of stones for drainage
18 in (45 cm)
Plastic sheet

Using the same materials as the captive system, the box is filled to within a few inches of its top. A damp sack is again needed as a cover that allows the passage of air and moisture. The success of any wormery depends on the quality of food and living conditions. Keep up a steady supply of kitchen scraps and periodically, say at two month intervals, add a fresh stock of manure and mature worms. Never let the farm become too wet. The worms will suffer and your relationships with neighbours may deteriorate if the smell becomes intolerable. The ideal conditions are a controlled dampness.

An occasional inspection of the worms will show whether they are breeding successfully. Remove all dead and sickly worms as they will soon contaminate the wormery and kill off the healthy lobs. It is possible, with care and a little luck, to provide lobworms throughout the year. Only excess dampness and hard frost will disturb the breeding process and both factors can be guarded against.

Redworms, the match angler's choice

Within the farmyard manure heap, under any fallen tree, or in damp areas hidden from the sun you will find the small redworm. Slender, lively and rarely more than 4 in (11.4 cm) long, this worm has the colour and movement to attract many species of fish. Most commercial worm farms breed this species for sale to anglers. The breeding cycle of the redworm is much faster than that of the larger lobworm and it lacks that awful penetrating smell associated with the brandling. Redworms can be

Above left *Lively, slender, the redworm lives in the rotting vegetation of the forest floor or the farmyard manure heap.* Above and right *Redworm colonies can be found in dungheaps by lifting the top layers with a fork. Then search the exposed areas for the entwined balls of whitish, juvenile redworms ideal for introducing into your own wormery of which kind you want.*

easily bred by the angler, using exactly the same worm farming methods, and are probably more easily kept than the lob.

The redworm thrives on a basic diet of pig manure, while the lob seems to prefer well-rotted horse manure. Getting the wormery started is again easy as all you need is permission to dig from a farm midden. Try to find the balls of white, immature worms that can be acclimatised to your habitat. Again, regular inspection is vital to remove dead worms and to monitor the amount of food that is being eaten by the worm colony. Redworms are prolific breeders, so unless worms are removed regularly for fishing the numbers will outgrow the wormery.

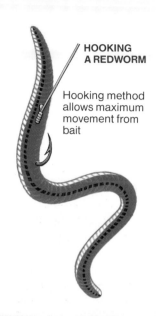

HOOKING A REDWORM

Hooking method allows maximum movement from bait

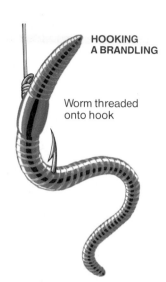

HOOKING A BRANDLING

Worm threaded onto hook

Fishing with the redworm

This small worm is an ideal trotting bait. It is lively on the hook, and can be used singly or as a small bunch. Hook size used will depend on the number and size of redworms. A hook of 12–16 size will be right in most conditions. When using a single worm the hook can be threaded through part of the body. This is a far better method of baiting than piercing the hook directly through the worm, where a taking fish can tear the bait from your tackle. My preference is to hook the worm midway along its body allowing the head and tail to move more freely.

Redworms are often fished as a 'cocktail' bait. The worm is threaded onto the hook bend and the point tipped with a caster. Maggots also have a place when a dual bait is thought necessary. There is much to be said for fishing a redworm hookbait over a bed of loose-fed red casters. I have seen a fine catch of River Erne roach and bream taken using this hook and groundbaiting combination.

The brandling

The third of the angler's worms looks very similar to the redworm with the addition of a series of yellow rings circling the body from just behind the creature's head to the tip of its tail. If there is anything that quickly identifies the brandling it is the obnoxious smell given off by this worm. The smell is readily transmitted onto the hands, possibly leading to the worm losing popularity as a bait.

Brandlings are found in similar habitats to the redworm. A well-established farmyard manure heap, will produce a regular supply of brandlings. Avoid using semi-liquid manure in your brandling worm-ery as the heap needs to be drying and well rotted. I much prefer this worm as a trotted bait. Fish get only a quick look at the bait as it passes, so have little chance to be deterred by any smell. I do not recommend the brandling as a legered, static bait. Fish could be put off by a close inspection, although the liveliness of the worm may well overcome a fish's natural suspicion of any unusual object.

Transporting worms

To be any good as a hookbait, worms must travel in a container that gives them air and a reasonably low temperature. They should never be carried in an airtight receptacle nor in the basic material of the wormery. Clean your worms for a few days before the fishing trip by moving them

Above left A single-hook rig for redworm (left) and a similar rig for the brandling (right). Both hold the creature securely while allowing the worm to wriggle attractively. Left A worm container should be non-metalic and be well ventilated.

to a clean container filled with sphagnum moss. The kind of stuff that florists sell to hold the water for flower bowls is ideal as it remains damp over long periods as well as cleansing the worms of all food and manure particles adhering to their bodies. Now, although the worms are clean they will have nothing to eat, so don't keep them any longer than a couple of days in moss. Those not used on the day should be returned immediately to the farm. If your trip is an extended one, perhaps a week's fishing in Ireland, the worms should not be scoured at all. Carry them in a large container with enough of the feed to keep them thick and healthy throughout your holiday.

A well-appointed worm container can be easily made by punching air holes in the lid of a clean plastic ice cream bucket, the sort that one gets from a supermarket. Alternatively, the modern emulsion paint container can be used, but it *must* be well cleaned to remove all traces of paint. Keep your worms out of direct sunlight when on the bank even if they are surrounded by a large wad of moss. Summer heat will soon dry the moss out and with it the worms. They'll quickly go lethargic and stringy and no longer form an attractive hookbait.

Maggot baits

The best known and most used bait for the coarse angler is the commercially-bred maggot, the product of different species of flies. The commonest maggot, available in a variety of artificially produced colours, is bred from bluebottle flies. Pinkies come from the greenbottle and squatts are the larvae of the common housefly. The parent or 'stud' flies are housed in a shed into which food, in the form of fish offal or condemned meat, is introduced. The action of flies laying their eggs on the flesh is described as 'blowing'. Depending on temperature, the eggs hatch in a few days. The tiny maggots begin feeding on the waste flesh which is removed from the fly shed into a growing-on house. New supplies of flesh are added according to the voracious appetite of the grubs. In the meantime, the cycle begins all over again for the mature breeding flies. Many millions of them are kept during their useful breeding life of about 13 weeks.

The maggots grow and build up in their bodies a reservoir of food that will sustain them throughout the grub stage and into the chrysalis or caster form. You can see the food as a black, elongated, speck that moves within the body. This is a good indicator of the quality and age of the maggots. Without that speck maggots are almost at the end of their larval stage, and will soon begin to change into casters so beware of buying grubs too long off the feed.

Commercially produced maggots are cleaned by introducing them

Commercially bred maggots being cleaned on shakers. Called riddling, it is also essential for the home maggot-breeder.

into trays of sawdust. They wriggle through the dust, which absorbs grease and removes particles of food from their bodies. It is debatable whether this is vitally important from a fishing point of view. The grease and natural odours on food are something that fish must associate with a multitude of grubs that fall into the water. What is certain is that anglers feel more confident when fishing with carefully prepared hookbait. Apart from sawdust, ground maize meal is a perfect medium for cleaning and giving a polished effect to the maggots.

The maggot varieties

First, most common and the largest among the maggots is the commercial, or white. Bred from bluebottles, the eggs are laid on fish or meat offal which gives them a plump appearance as grubs. When fresh from the bait farm these maggots are soft skinned—and here is an immediate problem; the soft maggot can be easily split when it is being

put on the hook. But there is a correct way to hook the grub without damaging the body.

Take a close look at the maggot. The blunt end has a fringe through which the hook should be inserted. Never pierce the body of the maggot, the skin will split allowing the body material to ooze out. Obviously the choice of hook size and type are vital when seeking perfect presentation of a lively, wriggling maggot. Many hook patterns are available that will suit maggot fishing but just two criteria need to be considered in selecting the right hook: it should be fine to medium in wire thickness and the point as sharp as possible. A single maggot can be fished on any hook size between 16 and 22. The size of the hook is relative to both the maggot and the expected fish. When using two maggots on a hook, I would extend the hook size to 14. This is a larger iron, balanced between the bulk of two grubs and the size of fish that the hook will handle.

The matter of bait in relation to hook size is an important one. Too large a hook will kill the maggot quickly and allow the fish to see a large iron. On the other hand, a hook that is too small for a largish bait allows a taking fish to rip the bait off the tiny hook without actually taking the baited hook into its mouth.

Left *White maggots, bred commercially in millions from the bluebottle, are the mainstay of coarse angling baits.* Below *Hook a single maggot at the frilled, blunt end. The head is at the other, pointed, end.*

MULTI-MAGGOT BAIT

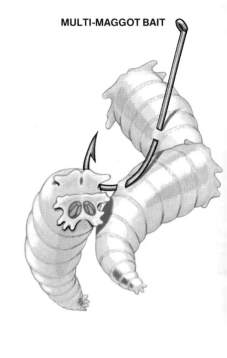

HOOKING A SINGLE MAGGOT

Above *How to assemble a multi-maggot hook bait.*

There are times when maggots fished as a multi-bait are required. Tench, carp, barbel and chub are species that will be attracted to a bunched bait. Naturally, the hook size has to be adjusted to take account of the fish's strength and body weight. I've had as many as a dozen maggots jammed onto a size 8 hook. It is inevitable that only a few of the larvae are really active as most of them are nicked through the centre of their bodies. The necessity for a lively-actioned maggot is less criticial in this form of bait presentation. The angler relies on the fish's greed for a big mouthful to overcome the possible lack of movement from the hookbaits.

Feeder maggots: the pinkie

The angler's maggot baits form two categories; those primarily used as hookbaits, and the baits used to feed fish within the swim or attract fish into fishing range. Feeder maggots are smaller than the commercial hook maggot. Bred from the greenbottle fly, their name comes from the delicate rose-pink colour of the grubs. Only about half the size of a commercial maggot, they can be used on small hooks as a change bait when the fishing is tough, or used as an attractor and loosefed into the swim.

The most useful attribute of the pinkie is that it is very active. Most fish feed by sight and are constantly looking for movement in the water. Having seen that movement in food animals, their senses of taste and smell enable them to find food among the bottom debris. When loose fed into the swim, pinkies sink gradually through the water, wriggling as they fall. Unfortunately, when they reach the bottom they quickly disappear among the debris. The value of this bait, therefore, is in being seen by fish as the pinkies sink rather than as providing a groundbait. The pinkie comes into its own when fish are feeding in midwater. Taking fish 'on the drop' can be achieved by fishing a single maggot on almost weightless tackle accompanied by a few pinkies loose-fed per cast.

The squatt

The smallest of the popular shop-bought maggots is bred from the common housefly. Squatts are a sedentary grub, lacking the activity shown by the pinkie. The value of this bait lies in loosefeeding an extremely small feeder maggot that will lie on the bottom in clear view of feeding fish. The squatt will not quickly disappear among the leaves and detritus that forms the bottom of most lakes and rivers.

Squatts can either be fed out onto the water where they sink rather more slowly than the pinkie—an added advantage when fishing on the drop—or they can be mixed into a cereal groundbait to provide a concentrated bottom feed. I have never used squatts on the hook, but they may well have a use as a change bait when conditions are tough.

Above right *Pinkies are maggots bred from greenbottle flies. They are used as feeders to attract fish and hold them in the swim.*
Above, far right *Smallest of the feeder maggots, the small wiry squatts are best kept in damp, red foundry sand. Small hooks, down to No. 22, are necessary for this tiny maggot.* Right *Comparative sizes of the common maggot baits. Commercials are the largest, pinkies smaller and livelier while squatts are the tiny, near-motionless grubs. All have their uses for anglers.*

Day 1A

Breeding gozzers can be done by any angler. They are cheap to produce and make an ideal bait. A sheep's heart is cleaned and sliced to provide access to egg-laying flies.

Day 1B

Place the heart on a piece of wood in the container. Cover the bottom of the container with a 2 in (5 cm) layer of bran. Seal the tub with clingfilm, pierced by a single hole. Put in a dark place.

Specials

Not all maggots can be regarded as commercial in production. The specials are either improved maggots bred from the bluebottle or those produced from other fly species. The gozzer, so often talked about but rarely seen by most coarse anglers, is a maggot that has been bred from a close relative of the bluebottle. For the amateur breeder the fly has a unique property. It blows in darkness, whereas most other flies lay their eggs in the light. This makes the gozzer an ideal maggot for the coarse angler to breed.

Gozzers are large, plump and soft maggots. They can be grown on at least two forms of feed. For home production I would choose the sheep's heart method. Breeding gozzers is not at all difficult using this system.

Day 1C

Attracted by the odours coming from the flesh of the heart, the gozzer fly arrives, eventually finding its way through the small hole in the clingfilm. There, it 'blows'—lays its eggs— on the heart.

Day 2

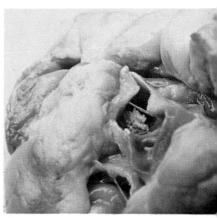

The eggs deposited by the gozzer fly can be seen in a neat cluster deep in one of the slits cut into the sheep's heart. Only allow one, at the most two, blows, then seal the container.

The picture sequence above shows you how to set about it.

You will need a large plastic container, such as an ice cream box, but a plastic bucket will do. Put a layer of bran in the bin, a few inches is enough. Buy a sheep's heart from the butcher. One is enough to provide enough gozzer hookbaits for a good day's fishing. With a sharp kitchen knife make four or five deep cuts across the heart. The idea is to let the maggots penetrate into where the best food is! Put the heart into the container, resting it on a roof tile or a block of wood. Doing this serves no purpose other than to make the removal of the heart for inspection a clean and easy thing to do.

You need a tight-fitting lid with a 1 in (2.5 cm) diameter hole in it. This provides an entrance for the bluebottle fly. Put the container into a

Day 3

Day 4

The tiny maggots have hatched out and begun to feed. As they eat their way deep into the sheep's heart they begin to grow fat and lively.

Another prepared sheep's heart. This one was not sealed off quickly enough and other flies deposited their eggs. One heart cannot provide enough food for maggots from multiple blows.

garage or potting shed out of all direct light. There doesn't have to be total darkness, just a very low light level. If you want to see what is happening without having to take the lid off, disturbing the contents, cover the container with cling-film.

If there are bluebottles about, one will enter the container and blow the fresh meat. Give the set-up at least two days before making your inspection. If there has been a blow, seen as a tiny cluster of whitish, elongated eggs, close the entrance to the lid to prevent any more flies getting inside. One heart will only feed the maggots from one blow.

Depending on the ambient temperature, the eggs will hatch in 2–6 days. The grubs will work their way deep into the heart feeding voraciously. Within three days you will have to give them further food as their appetites are truly enormous. Some breeders introduce a little soft,

Day 8

Fully grown maggots begin to emerge from the nearly eaten heart. As they stop feeding they drop off into the bran and cleanse themselves as they wriggle through it.

Day 9

Fat, juicy gozzers provide one of the finest maggot hookbaits. Maggots like these, and fished with the correct style and expertise, have accounted for many specimen fish.

brown sugar at this stage believing that it gives an increased succulence to the gozzers. Feeding will finish at about the fifth or sixth day. At that time the maggots will leave what remains of the meat, dropping down into the bran.

When all maggots have left the heart they will need riddling to clean them of stickiness. A quick swish around a bait tin with some added maize meal will give you a perfectly clean and polished hookbait. Don't attempt to store gozzers for more than a couple of days. They soon develop toughened skins which destroy their value as the prized hookbait that the gozzer has become. With careful planning, the sheep's heart can be laid down to produce gozzers when you want them. In summer weather a heart, properly blown, will provide you with maggots eight days later.

Day 1A

To breed milkfly maggots, mix bran into a smooth, if unpleasant porridge by adding a mixture of cabbage water and sour milk.

Day 1B

Half fill a plastic container with the mixture. This provides both food and a perfect environment for the milkfly maggots. Place the tub in a dark place and await the fly specifically attracted to the mixture.

The milkfly or sour bran maggot

Another special that can be easily produced by the angler is the milkfly or sour bran maggot. Breeding this grub is simple and in use easily rivals the gozzer as a fish taker. In appearance there is a similarity to the latter except that the sour bran specials are smaller and a pure white in colour, forming a most attractive, active hookbait.

Breeding them is simple. Start with a container similar to that used for gozzers. Measure out enough fine bran to half fill the bin. Add milk, sour if there is any in the kitchen, and the water drained from cooking cabbage. About a 50 per cent mixture of liquid to solid is about right. Pour the liquid over the bran and stir to a sloppy, porridge-like consistency. Keep the container in a similar situation to that for gozzer production. Sour bran specials are the product of a secretive fly that also blows in low light conditions.

Days 14–18

Check that the blow has occurred by lifting the crust that has formed in the semi-liquid mixture. The eggs or tiny larvae will be seen in the cracks that have formed in the material just below the surface.

Day 22

The maggots are ready. Rinse the mixture away through a fine sieve to leave the maggots. Clean them in dry bran and hold in a maggot container. If the fishing trip is not for a day or so, keep it in the fridge.

All we have to do now is wait for the flies to visit the maggot farm. There seems to be some difference of opinion about the length of time taken for the flies to lay their eggs. I think it depends on the sourness of the food mixture. It seems that the adult fly requires a certain smell to enable it to find the feed.

After a few days in a summer temperature the upper layer of bran will dry out, leaving a maze of narrow cracks across the surface. Any fly attracted to the container will lay its eggs down into the cracks. Inspection of the container will show if there has been a blow, although accurate detection is sometimes difficult. Those experienced in maggot breeding will tell you to put your ear to the box and listen for the sounds made by feeding maggots! These creatures are fairly large, very active, and can make an audible noise. It is important not to break the crust until the maggots are needed as bait. This species of maggot takes a lot longer to reach bait size than the gozzer, so allow at least two weeks in the height of summer from the time that the blow is seen.

Both gozzers and sour bran specials are maggots of the summer. They are hard to breed in the cooler months and virtually impossible in the winter. Also, the gozzer stiffens up in cold water, giving it the appearance of a stretched commercial grub.

There are other maggot specials but they are difficult to breed and not absolutely vital for the purpose of fishing. Match men are the anglers who devise all manner of alternative baits in the hope that one special or other will give them the edge in competition. Here, I have concentrated on the two maggots that can be fairly easily produced by the average angler. There is always a danger that we become involved in the mysteries of maggot breeding to the detriment of our fishing!

LIFE-CYCLE OF THE BLUEBOTTLE

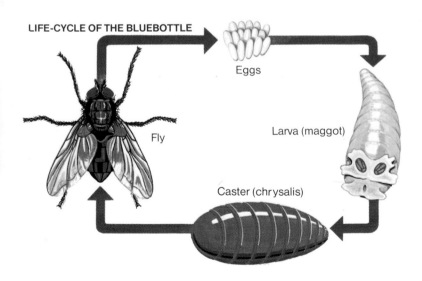

Eggs

Larva (maggot)

Fly

Caster (chrysalis)

The life cycle of the bluebottle, and other flies: egg-grub-chrysalis-adult fly.

Casters

Flies of any species have four distinct stages in their lives. The mature fly lays its eggs, which hatch into maggots or grubs. After a feeding period the grub becomes a chrysalis (known to anglers as a 'caster') during which time the outer skin hardens into a dark-brown case. Development continues until the adult fly splits the case to emerge as a fully-winged insect.

The success of casters as a hookbait comes from the experiences of roach anglers during the 1950s. As with most bait developments, the match anglers of the North proved that the caster is a superb roach bait. There are anglers who consider it a better all-river bait than the live maggot. Either way, it is a bait that most running-water fishermen should not want to be without.

HOOKING A CASTER

Hide the entire hook within the caster

When fishing the caster, the hook must be hidden entirely inside the chrysalis, or caster. Hook it carefully or the pupa case will split.

Stage 1

To produce your own casters, start with 1½ pints of good-quality maggots.

Stage 2

Spread the maggots evenly over a 2 in (5 cm) deep layer of white wood sawdust.

Of course, casters can be bought from the tackle shop. They are slightly more expensive than maggots as their production is far more involved and must be timed to suit weekend fishing demands. Turning shop-bought maggots into casters is a simple task. To provide a pint of casters you will need to have about 1½ pints of white maggots. Start the process by buying fresh maggots, those with an evident black speck rippling within the body. Riddle them to remove the sawdust and any waste matter carried over from the bait farm.

You will need some shallow trays (kitchen baking tins are ideal), to hold the turning maggots. After riddling, spread maggots across the surface of a couple of inches of clean, white-wood sawdust. Again a garage or potting shed will give the conditions of low light and not too much heat that will ensure perfect turning of the casters. At average summer temperatures, say 65° F (18.3° C), the maggots will take about a week to turn. Much depends on their condition and the prevailing

Stage 3

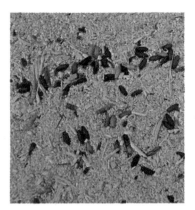

Kept in low light at about 65°F (18°C) the maggots will soon begin to turn. Riddle to get the first batch and avoid dead maggots.

Stage 4

Wash the chrysalids in water. Discard the floaters, keeping only those that sink. Floaters take fish out of the swim.

weather, so one's timing cannot be exact.

The turning process will be gradual, not all maggots becoming chrysalids at the same time. Now comes the hard work. The contents of each tray will have to be riddled twice a day. As the casters are taken off they must be cleansed and rinsed with clean water to remove all traces of rubbish. Put the casters into plastic bags and pack down tight, without crushing, and seal the bags to make them airtight. The casters are then stored in a refrigerator at just above freezing point. This temperature is vital, don't put the casters into the freezer compartment.

It is wise to dry out casters on a cloth before packing them away. If there is too much moisture in the plastic bag, the casters may go sour. Fish can detect soured casters and they leave them severely alone. Freshly bagged casters have an almost indefinite fridge life. Providing the temperature is kept at 32°F (1–2°C), casters will stay fit to fish with as all development of the flies has been suspended.

Stage 5

As the maggots begin to turn, they must be riddled twice a day to remove the unwanted floaters.

Stage 6

Store the cleaned casters in polythene bags. Keep them in the fridge at 2° above zero °C or 32°F.

Fishing with casters

When caster fishing the hooking method is dictated by the speed that fish snatch the bait. A caster that is nicked onto the hook will be stripped off with hardly a movement of the float. The hook must be buried within the caster. This is done by inserting the point of the hook into the large, rounded end of the body. As the point penetrates the chrysalis, the hook shank is swung up in an arc. The hook is then pushed down inside the caster until only the whipped shank or hook eye is left emerging. Fish have to see the bait clearly and then take it confidently into their mouths. A badly-hooked caster swinging from the hookbend is a gift to a hungry fish. The only time a caster is nicked onto the hook is when fishing maggot and caster as a cocktail. Then the maggot is attached to wriggle freely at the bend with the caster covering the hookpoint and barb.

Only sinkers are wanted when you fish with casters. The difference between floating and sinking casters cannot reliably be judged by the

Above *Riddles made of plastic can be kept in a maggot box. The wire basket-type, bought from most hardware stores, fits a plastic bucket. Their mesh size is ideal for maggots. Pinkies require a small mesh, similar to the perforated zinc sheets used to ventilate domestic larders.* Below *White commercially bred maggots can be coloured by adding powdered dye to water. The coloured water is then poured over white-wood sawdust and the maggots become coloured as they crawl through it. When they have reached the required tint, the maggots must be put into clean sawdust to make them remove excess dye. Some dyes may be harmful to the skin.*

eye. But it is easy to sort out the sinkers by dropping the casters into a bucket of water at the waterside. Floaters are casters undergoing the metabolic process that lightens the pupa as the fly is being formed. The sinker is newly turned, with the body juices having a similar weight to that of the maggot. Floaters can be thrown out onto the surface of the water as an indicator of the presence of mid-water fish. These will rise to the bait, but such fish tend to follow wind-blown or current-blown floaters out of your swim. .

Dyeing maggots

It is not known why fish prefer different coloured maggots over a period of time. It is possible that a coloured maggot resembles something that the fish finds naturally. Over the years, attempts have been made to produce a coloured hookbait that has a greater attractiveness. There are two ways to colour maggots: colour feeding, in which the maggot takes in food that gives colour right through the body; or introducing dye to sawdust in which the maggots are moving. Annatto, a harmless additive to dairy products, is added to the carcases on which the maggots feed. Absorbing this colouring via the feed gives the annatto maggot a delicate yellow tinge.

Maggots can be fed with powdered dye. The dyes can be bought from a number of sources including tackle shops and result in the following colours:

Chrysodine	Bronze-yellow
Chrysodine R	Reddish-bronze
Rhodamine	Pink
Auromine	Yellow

Most of us buy our maggots from the tackle dealer. He may well dye commercial maggots to suit the requirements of his customers. These maggots are generally dyed after the grub has finished feeding. You may find when buying coloured maggots that the dye comes off onto your hands. The reason for this is that the maggots' skins are coloured by the dye which in liquid form has been added to the sawdust through which the maggots are constantly moving. After the grubs have achieved the desired colour they are placed in clean whitewood sawdust and left to scour themselves of excess colouring. Usually, little dye is transferred to the angler's hands.

In the angling press recently there has been considerable controversy about chrysodine. There is a suggestion that this dye may be a cause of cancer among humans. Quite naturally, anglers are concerned as they, more than any other section of the population, use this particular dye to

Above *Bronze, red, yellow and white maggots. These are the
standard colours achieved by dyeing commercially bred grubs.*
Below *Some of the wide range of bait boxes available, made in
plastic. They must have adequate ventilation holes in the lid, which
should fit tightly.*

provide the popular bronze maggot. Evidence of the concern over maggot dyes is shown by a statement by ICI that no dye, even those used for food colouring, would be recommended for colouring bait in the way anglers use it. Take care, then, when considering colouring maggots.

Transporting maggots

There are two occasions when anglers take maggots on fishing trips: the couple of pints for a day's pleasure fishing or the more complicated business of a larger amount of maggots needed for something like a fishing holiday in Ireland. The former situation presents no bait problems. There are a multitude of suitable maggot boxes on the market, and all keep the bait in superb condition for at least a few days. The requirements are simple. The box must be secure, nobody wants maggots wandering in the boot of the car! There must be adequate ventilation, and the holes must not become blocked. In my opinion, it is sound commonsense to put one pint of maggots in a box designed to accommodate a quart. The extra space is needed for bran or sawdust to keep the maggots cool.

Boxes should never be packed one above the other. The ventilation holes are in the lids so carrying them in this fashion will ensure the asphixiation of maggots in the lower boxes. Maggots generate a lot of heat, which needs dissipating. They are an expensive bait so treat them

An insulated maggot container, with freezer packs to keep the bait in perfect condition during trips needing days of travel.

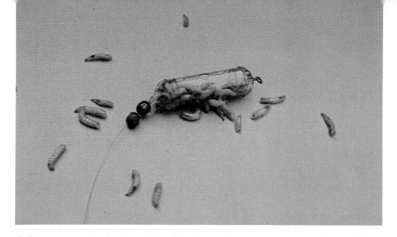

A Drennan swimfeeder offers little resistance to current flow. The weight can be added or subtracted in the form of swan shots.

kindly. A longer journey or when one has to preserve maggots over a period of time, calls for a specialized container. A friend of mine, Trevor King, who is both a tackle dealer and an importer of tropical fish, has provided the answer. His tropical fish arrive in Britain within a large polystyrene box. It will just take two one-gallon ice cream cartons leaving sufficient space to add at least eight freezer packs. The kind of thing that is sold to keep a picnic salad and its accompanying bottle of wine cool.

We pack the maggots with at least their bulk of finely-sifted sawdust. No lids are put on the individual cartons as the maggots need to breathe. The ice packs keep the temperature down to the low thirties F. Adhesive tape is stuck around the box and its lid to prevent escapes. Incidentally, enough air passes through the polystyrene to keep the grubs alive. Only the amount of maggots needed for one day's fishing are taken from the container at a time. When the ice-packs lose their chill they should be washed and taken to the kitchen hotel or guesthouse for refreezing. There is no smell providing the ice-packs are washed and I've never had my requests refused. Perhaps it is because I have never told the hotel staff where the packs had been. . . !

Controlled feeding with maggots
Maggots are efficient fish attractors. They wriggle invitingly on a hook, can be thrown or catapulted to a selected area of water as loosefeed; they can be mixed with cereal bait to form a stodgy mixture that can be placed on the bed of a river with great accuracy. Sometimes the fishing style

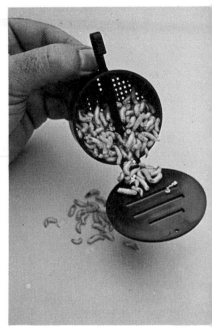

demands that the loosefeed be placed within inches of the hookbait. Legering is one fishing system that can be used to carry the fish-attracting loosefeed to exactly the lie of the hookbait. The reason is simple—the two are cast together.

Anglers have developed a number of containers for both groundbait and maggots, called swimfeeders, that are attached to the terminal rig. Combinations of the two baits can also be catered for by plugging the open feeder at both ends with stiff groundbait, thus trapping the maggots between the cereal.

Baitdroppers are another means of getting any form of loosefeed down to where fish are. They operate on the basis that the feed is contained within a compartment that opens when the dropper reaches the bed of the river or lake. Baitdroppers do not have the accuracy of placing that we associate with the swimfeeder but they have their uses when we need to put bait in a defined position on the bottom. Thrown or catapulted feed would be a lot less accurate.

Above, far left *The bait-dropper is loaded with maggots, its lid held shut by the lead weight.* Top left *When the bait-dropper hits the riverbed the weight releases its pressure on the lid which opens and releases the bait.* Above *Alan Edwards loosefeeding with an angler's catapult, an accurate method.* Right *Catapult pouches of different shapes for different uses. The two cups are intended for groundbait, while the pouches accommodate maggots without them falling out before or during catapulting.*

The bloodworm

There has probably been more controversy about bloodworms than any other bait. It has been banned from use in many match fishing circles because on the one hand it is successful and on the other it is difficult to obtain. Bloodworm is sold in some tackle shops but, generally, it is a hookbait that must be collected by the angler. The bans on its use result from the fact that collecting bloodworm is incredibly hard and dirty work. Not every angler has the inclination to engage in that form of activity and matchwinners, using bloodworm, have found themselves castigated for *having the edge* on their fellows rather than being admired for their skill in finding and gathering the bait.

Bloodworms are the larvae of the midge. Smaller larvae, called jokers, are produced by the gnat. I shall deal with both baits together because their uses and value to the angler are similar. Without doubt both baits can be considered as matchmen's gear. The bloodworm is found among the soft ooze that forms the bed of lakes, ponds and canals. It tolerates a high degree of pollution. In fact, the first place to look for them is in any stagnant water known to be polluted. The traditional farm pond, into which pig manure leaches, provides the perfect habitat for bloodworms so long as the pollution doesn't reach massive proportions.

Bloodworms can be collected throughout the year, with a short period, happily during the latter half of the close season, when they rise up through the water to hatch into the winged insect. This explosion of life, then, reveals the presence of the bloodworm. For, as the larval form undergoes its metamorphosis many thousands of empty nymphal shells are left lying on the surface of the water.

The larvae are collected with the aid of a simple tool, a metal bar which can be bound to the end of a hoe handle. Gathering bloodworms involves wading deep into the pond. Waders may suffice but I recommend chest-high waders as there may be the odd hole into which one can drop and the job is a dirty one that needs maximum personal protection. A container, either attached to the angler's belt or in the form of a floating tray, keeps both hands free for the job of scraping the bottom. This is done by a sweeping motion of the tool, bringing the blade through the mud an inch or so down into the soft mud. The sweep is continued, out of the mud and up through the water. Any bloodworms present will be found sticking across the metal blade. They are then wiped off by running the blunt metal through thumb and forefinger and deposited into the container.

Jokers are somewhat harder to find. Unlike the larger bloodworm, the joker is a creature of rivers and streams. It is not found in stillwater. The first place to look for them is in a slightly polluted river, well downstream of the source of the pollution. Use the same scraper-tool, making trial scrapes until the presence of this minute larva is detected.

Bloodworms are used as hookbait. The smaller and more lively jokers are added to ground and cloudbait to act as fish attractors. This bait is highly prized by bream anglers for its value in holding fish within the swim. Small, fine-wire hooks size 20 are the right kind for a bunch of four larvae. Each bloodworm is attached by nicking the hook through behind the head.

BLOODWORM SCRAPER

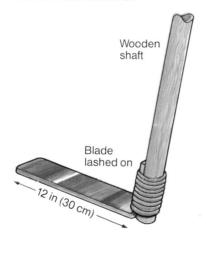

Wooden shaft

Blade lashed on

12 in (30 cm)

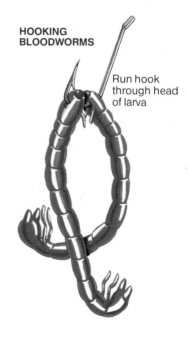

HOOKING BLOODWORMS

Run hook through head of larva

Above *A bloodworm scraper made of a steel bar lashed to the handles of a hoe.* Right *The tiny bloodworm is hooked through the head.*

A bait that is difficult to gather deserves looking after. Clean bloodworms by gently swishing them round in a bowl of water. Try to get rid of as much mud as possible. Drain off the water through a piece of fine net, a woman's stocking is ideal. The larvae will be massed in a ball, and should be dropped onto a quantity of finely-sifted garden peat. Here, they will separate, and crawl into the medium. The peat sold for improving lawns is perfect and dark black in colour. It is an alternative to the matchman's 'Black Magic', a North of England introduction to angling described as the leaf mould produced by the breakdown of rhododendron leaves. Jokers are best kept in the same material. Now wrap the worms and peat in sheets of newspaper so that they can breath. Closed bait boxes are not really suitable. Both baits will keep well in a refrigerator, set at a temperature suitable for maggots.

Mealworms

Most pet shops can supply this grub (the larval stage of a beetle), which can be offered as a change bait when trotting for chub or roach. Slightly larger than a gozzer, they have rather tough skins, which makes them a last-resort bait. I have had success with mealworms in Denmark, where my maggots stretched in the unbelievable heat. At that time maggots were not available, but a friend bought some mealworms from a cage bird dealer. Those Danish roach took our mealworms greedily.

Wasp grubs

Matchmen, particularly those who fish for chub, will go to any lengths to get wasp grubs and the nest material. Because of the nature of wasps, getting their grubs is a dangerous pastime. Acute eyesight is demanded as the nest has to be found. Having established where it is, leave it alone until very late in the evening. Nests are either underground, in a hedgerow bank or built in a gap between walls. It will have to be dug out and to do that the wasps must be killed. There are a number of poisons, mostly in powder form, that will do this. Unfortunately, at least one of them—Cymag—contains cyanide, and it is dangerous stuff! When wet, the danger is increased as it gives off cyanide gas.

The powder, placed on the end of a long wooden batten, is introduced to the nest entrance. Additional powder must be spread around the immediate vicinity. Be careful to read and understand the directions accompanying the wasp poison, especially those concerned with the time taken to kill the nest's occupants. I'm in favour of using one of the non-poisonous insect killers sold at most chemists which contain the African chemical pyrethrum. It's the chemical contained in fly sprays.

Try to get every scrap of material that forms the nest, as it is as valuable in fishing terms as the grubs. Wasp grubs are large and soft, giving a perfect presentation on hooks of 14-16 size. Avoid the extremely fine-wire irons from which the grub is easily torn. There are two different sizes of wasp larvae, the small worker grubs and larger queen grubs. The smaller larvae are suitable to be mounted as a double on a 14 hook. The nest material has the taint of the sweet food that the grubs are fed on. When pulverised and with boiling water added it forms a 'cake'. This, mixed with brown crumb, forms a superb groundbait that will attract fish in a way few others do.

Docken grubs

If you search around the roots of the common dock plant it is quite likely that you will unearth a large, brownish caterpillar with a red head that

Mealworms are the grubs of a beetle found in flour mills.

has a clear black point to it. It is the product of a ghost moth and can be found all over Britain up to May, when it forms a chrysalis that becomes a moth in July. From this you will see that the juicy grub is of little use to summer fishermen. But in autumn the grub makes a good dapping lure for chub and big roach. Its only drawback is that the docken grub has a very soft skin that tears easily.

Caterpillars and insects

Walk any river on a warm evening and you will see the feeding activities of many species of fish. The dimpled surface and broadening rings indicate the presence of a feeding fish taking insects or falling grubs. Millions of insects and their larvae fall into our fishing waters during any season. The trout angler recognizes this and his artificial lures are tied to accurately represent the rain of food that falls on the surface.

There are particular times when the game angler realizes that his artificial is no match for the real thing. He will then attempt to dap the

Below The docken grub is the caterpillar of the ghost moth. Below right Caddis larvae and small creatures such as caterpillars and other insects make excellent coarse fish baits. Below far right Bread is a versatile bait, providing both hookbait and groundbait.

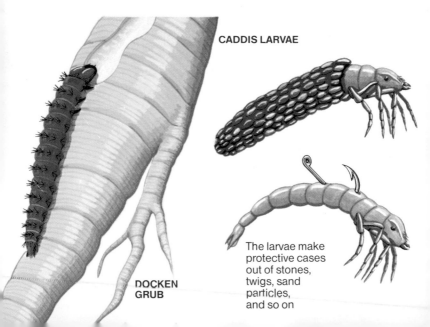

CADDIS LARVAE

DOCKEN GRUB

The larvae make protective cases out of stones, twigs, sand particles, and so on

natural creature. Coarse fishers would do well to follow this example. Beetles, moths, caterpillars, flies, grasshoppers and a hundred other species can be used, either as the insect or the larval form. Some are easy to find by just pulling up a tussock of grass or digging among the dead leaves at the base of trees. There is great angling satisfaction in floating them down on a greased, free-line tackle or a tiny trotting float to fish that lie open-mouthed for the inevitable falling food.

Bread baits

There was a time when all newcomers to fishing used some form of bread as their bait to learn with. It will take almost all coarse fish, with the possible exception of the predators although there are times when even a pinch of flake has encouraged a pike to attack! It is a handy bait, easy to come by and neatly packaged. Each new, crusty loaf will provide three beautiful types of hookbait. The outer crust, apart from the blackest domed part of the loaf, makes a good floating bait either torn as an irregular piece or cut into neat, hook-sized squares. The soft inner part of the loaf gives us flake and when a few days old the same inner textured material can be used to make paste.

Bread crusts as bait

Crust has an inherent buoyancy which we can usefully employ to fish for

BREAD BAITS

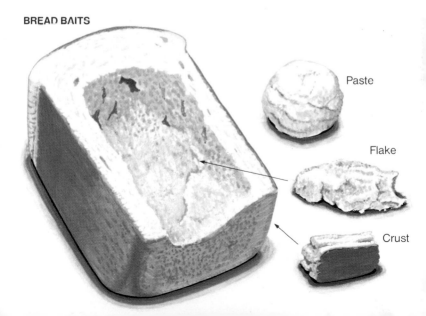

Paste

Flake

Crust

Preparing crust hookbait

Cut off the side of a tin loaf—but beware, the bandaged finger in the photograph is evidence of the danger of sharp knives used carelessly.

Press the crust between boards to aid in cutting accurate evenly-shaped hook-sized pieces.

Surface crust bait: briefly dip the soft side of a crust into water. It will then absorb enough weight to be cast out to the swim without the addition of unnecessary lead on the terminal tackle.

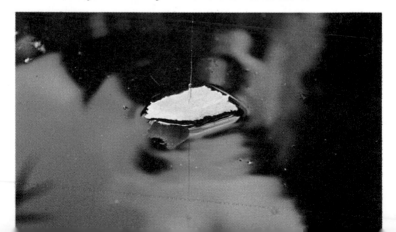

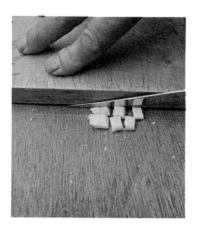

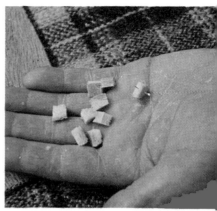

Inch-square crusts need a No. 8 hook. Use size 14, with ½ in squares for roach and size 2, with 1 in squares for carp.

A proven and attractive bait for all bottom-dwelling and midwater species.

those species that are surface or mid-water feeders. The problem is that the bait is virtually weightless which makes casting difficult. This can be overcome by dipping the hooked bait into the water for a few seconds to let the soft underside absorb some water. It will then cast with ease and yet retain that element of buoyancy so vital to the bait presentation.

Roach and rudd are two species that respond to crust baits. The average specimen is not of a large size, in fact the mouths of both fish are rather small. So, we fit the crust to the fish in order that it takes the bait positively without giving a series of false bites as it whittles a large piece down to takeable size. Many years ago Fred Buller, a man who has many fine roach to his credit, introduced me to his method. Before fishing, Fred spends an evening cutting perfectly shaped crusts suited to the fish he is seeking. This also cuts down the time spent tearing lumps from a loaf at the waterside. Fred adds that they should then be sealed in an airtight sweet jar and that they should be covered with a sprinkling of table salt to preserve them.

Balanced crust

There will come a time when you need a bait with controlled buoyancy, one that will sink slowly down to perhaps lie on a bed of soft bottom weed without disappearing into the vegetation. Such a bait can be obtained by pressing paste against the crust around the hook shank area. Control of the rate of sink, through the depths, is managed by varying the amount of paste or size of crust.

Flake

The soft, fluffy inner part of a fresh loaf gives us one of the fisherman's favourite baits. Pinched around the hook shank it casts well and swells rapidly when in the water. The bait is taken by most coarse fish in the warmer months of the year. As autumn comes we find that most fish refuse a large piece of flake but their interest can be re-awakened by the use of smaller baits. It is important how you apply the flake to your hook. Pinch the bread hard at the shank only, not around the hook bend or point. Bread does become hardened and a shrouded point may mean a lost fish, so try to keep the point just clear of the bread.

When fishing for the smaller species, or at times when fish are hard to hook, it is a good idea to resort to the bread punch. The material is still flake but it is punched out from sliced bread in a regular size that cannot be done with the fingers. The punches are sold with heads of different diameters so that bait proportions can be slightly varied to cope with different fish. A point in favour of using the bread punch is that any taint on the hands will not be transferred to the bread, because the fingers never touch the punch tip.

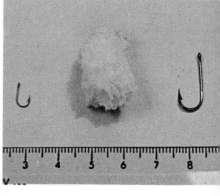

Far left *Press bread paste round the hook shank on the fluffy side of a crust to produce a balanced crust bait, shown in the next photograph.* Above *Lay the hard to cut a clean shape out of the bread.* Above right *Punched bread can be hooked off the punch without being handled.* Right *Bread flake must be matched to hook size. (Measure shows centimetres.)*

53

Long-casting situations, with big fish in mind, call for special attention to flake baits. It is no use trying to cast a pinched-on flake bait beyond a few rod lengths. However, fishing conditions may well demand flake fished at distance. The answer is to reduce the size of the bait in a bread press. This little vice can reduce a large lump of bread to about one eighth of its original bulk, making it a lot easier to cast. In addition, the bait soon swells up after a few moments in the water. I've found another use for the bread press: giving sufficient stiffness to soft, high protein baits that always seem to fly off when I'm casting.

Paste baits and how to make them

Probably the first bait used by any child coming to freshwater fishing, and still one of the best, paste is a bait that will stand comparison with any other made from bread. Two criteria must be observed though. The hook size must be absolutely right for a given size of paste droplet and the paste must be soft enough to allow the hook to pull through it without being so soft that it flies off during a lusty cast.

I fish paste on hooks between 6–16. A wide variation? True, but carp have a liking for large baits which need a matching hook, while roach and small chub need to be tempted with a tiny bait on the smaller hook. On the hook, I call the paste bait a droplet. That, for me, describes its shape perfectly. Gently mould the paste round the shank of the hook to leave the point just showing from the side of the bait.

Paste is made from slightly stale bread, a loaf about two days old is right. Cut off the crusts and soak the bread in water. Squeeze out as much water as you can and place the resultant mess in a muslin square. Wring the cloth firmly to get rid of further moisture. Now, comes the messy bit. The paste has to be continuously kneaded to get the correct

Left Paste must be shaped to leave the hook-point clear. Below Using the useful bread press to produce a hook-sized bait. It squeezes bread to a fraction of its normal size.

The preparation of good quality breadpaste

Tear the interior from the centre of a loaf, one of at least two days old, and wet it thoroughly.

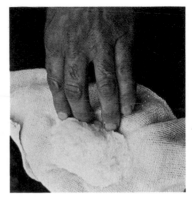

Wrap the wet bread in a piece of clean muslin cloth.

consistency—tacky. At this stage, if in squeezing the dough still sticks to your fingers, too much moisture still remains.

Now is the time to work into the paste any additives that you feel will help you to catch fish. Without doubt cheese, hemp dust, aniseed and custard powder (the vanilla flavouring), can all be fish attractors on their day. And, like maggots, some colouring may provide that little extra pulling power. I've experimented with cochineal (red cake colouring), custard powder (pale lemon) and Red Leicester cheese (orange) to give both colour and taste. There is no doubt that fish can detect waterborne tastes at considerable distances downstream of the angler. For this reason, I often match groundbait and hookbait with similar attractors.

Recently, we have seen the arrival of ready-mixed paste baits backed with matching groundbait systems. They work and take away the chore of mixing paste. A measured amount is simply wetted with plain water prior to judicious kneading. The additives are already within the mix and only enough for the fishing day need be made up.

Squeeze the muslin tight to remove as much moisture as possible.

Knead the dough until it is of a soft, tacky consistency. Keep the paste in an air-tight container.

CLOUDBAIT

Hookbait should sink through descending cloudbait

Top left *Use a plastic bowl to mix groundbait, pouring the dry crumb on to the water—not the other way round—to ensure a completely wetted mixture.* Above *Heavy feed should be compressed into balls that do not break up in the air while being thrown out into the swim. The feed must go down fast in the water to break up only when it reaches the bottom. This is the area where the angler needs to hold the fish. It is bad technique to allow feed to spread over a wide area.* Left *Cloudbait working in stillwater to encourage fish to gather.*

GROUNDBAIT

There are many forms of groundbait and a multitude of proprietary mixes are sold by tackle dealers together with the raw materials for anglers who mix their own. All these concoctions have two aims in mind: to entice fish into an angler's swim and to hold them there. We do this either by the cloudbait system, in which fish see the fine particles descending through the water, or with a bottom-feeding method where the bait lies static or drifts downstream. After many years of fishing activity fish are conditioned to groundbaiting.

Cloudbaiting

This method consists of a visual presentation of fine food particles to sub-surface and midwater fish, and is of particular importance during the warmer months when fish rise to feed on plankton and surface creatures. The food material can be brown or white crumb that has been finely ground and sifted. Start by putting water into a mixing bowl, or a simple plastic, round basin. Corners in a bowl are a heck of a nuisance, for the dry feed gets into the corners and sticks there. To ensure thorough wetting add the dry crumb to the water. Adding water to groundbait never achieves the same degree of wetting, the material at the bottom of the bowl will always stay dry. Try to obtain a damp, crumbly mix that can be firmed into egg-sized balls. These should be firm enough to throw, while giving immediate break-up as they hit the water. Try to achieve a rain of fine particles, slowly sinking down to the bottom. Additional attractiveness can be had by adding a small amount of cornflour or dried milk powder, both of which add a milky quality to the cloudbait as it sinks.

Groundbaiting the bottom

For this operation, our constituents are basically the same as for cloudbait except that you need a medium-ground crumb that will bind together to reach the bottom before breaking up to form a carpet of feed.

To do this, one must get sufficient water into the feed and ensure perfect dispersal. Correctly wetted, the groundbait will hit the water, sink, and only begin to break up as it nears the bottom. However, faced with a river that has a strong flow, the bait has to be got down quickly to ensure that it doesn't break up too fast, and kept within the swim, rather than 50 yards (46 m) below the angler's peg! Weight has to be added in the form of fine silver sand or earth. Sand will take the bait down fast with a slight break-up during the fall. Earth or mud binds the feed into a solid mass that sinks like a stone, to break up more slowly as the river current washes around it.

Steps in the preparation of groundbait

Stale loaves need to have the outer crusts cut away before being baked. This aids the even baking of the soft, inner areas.

After the crust is removed, the loaf should be baked at 200°F (93.3°C) for an hour or until it crushes easily.

Additions to the feed

Samples of the hookbait can be mixed into the bulk of the groundbait. Maggots, casters, worms, pieces of bread are easily introduced to sharpen the appetites of the fish. These are introduced after wetting and during the final mixing stage. Both pinkies and squatts can be added, the choice of which depends on the type of lake or river bottom; pinkies for a clean riverbed or squatts for a mucky bottom.

Over-groundbaiting can be worse than not feeding at all and this is especially so when we use a feed that has added attraction. Little and often is the time-honoured rule. Start by introducing a couple of balls into a chosen swim. Then start to fish. If bites follow regularly, throw a little more feed in but do it carefully. Don't bombard feeding fish with enormous lumps that hit the water with an explosive thump. When the bait has settled, avoid any more disturbance of the surface above their heads by casting the float or leger tackle to a point beyond the ground-

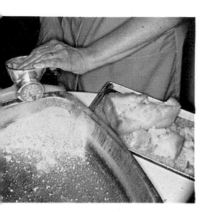

Break up the baked loaves and grind them through a kitchen mincer, at first with a coarse mince, then through a fine blade.

Use a kitchen sieve with fine mesh to remove lumps from the well-crushed crumb. The material should be of an even consistency.

baited area. Then draw the terminal rig back into the feed location.

Only one species will tolerate heavy groundbaiting while they are feeding and that is a shoal of bream that have begun to feed seriously. At first, it seems that they are scared by the amount of feed hitting the water, but soon lose their fear of the surface commotion. Bream anglers use the phrase 'getting their heads down' to describe the frenzy that a bream shoal displays when truly on the feed. And a lot of groundbait is needed to hold their interest. Bream are like sheep in that they graze an area bare in a very short time. The problem, then, is to give the fish enough food to encourage them to remain without scaring them off as the necessary groundbait goes in!

By mixing the feed at home the night before you can cut down time spent at the waterside in groundbait preparation. This has two benefits: the feed will be thoroughly wetted and you will achieve a consistency in groundbait quality difficult to get at the waterside.

Feeding the swim

As with loosefeeding, the float fisherman can either throw his groundbait manually or deliver it by means of a catapult. Legering with a swimfeeder enables us to place the groundbait exactly where we want it. Use an open-ended feeder packed with groundbait that will be washed out to flow around the hookbait when fishing in running water. Stillwater fishing requires a slightly different approach. The same swimfeeder rig is used but the groundbait is eased out of the feeder by gently striking after the rig has settled on the bottom. Another way to release groundbait from the swimfeeder is to add some maggots to the mix. The cereal feed will be pushed out from the feeder by the wriggling maggots.

It is important to get groundbait to the correct spot. Accurate groundbaiting can be achieved by the use of a swimfeeder.

Additives

Recently we have seen and heard of the use of high protein additives to baits both for the hook and for groundbait. Apart from the carp angler, who spends much time and energy devising special magical mixes for the specimen hunt, many of these so-called high protein additives can be found in the average family kitchen. Catfood, meat extracts, such as Marmite, sugar, dried blood, dried milk powder, are all taste additives that can give the edge on normal baiting procedures.

While colour is sometimes useful I generally rely on only two. Brown and white. These, given by the basic colouring of the crumb in use, seem to cover all situations. If anything, brown crumb seems to have a greater application. White crumb, possibly lying on a stark, dark-brown riverbed, seems to be less effective. No doubt fish are put off by the violent contrast between bait and background. The only time I've depended on white crumb is when fishing a canal that has a bed of glistening chalky clay. There the fish are turned off by any dark coloured feed.

In times gone by, anglers used additives with strong odour. Aniseed, cheese, and fish-oil are three additives that attracted fish. At least one British company has re-introduced both paste hookbait and groundbaits containing these natural materials.

Additives and hookbaits that can be found in most kitchens:	
Spaghetti	
Macaroni	
Bread	*All of these baits are cereal based*
Breakfast cereals	
Cat biscuits	
Rice	
Sausages	
Luncheon meat	*These baits are meat based, with the*
Dog food	*addition of cereals and protein additives*
Cat food	
Custard powder	*Essentially a bait flavouring (vanilla)*
Marmite	*A high protein based on yeast extracts*
Cheese	*Can be used as a hookbait or added to groundbaits for taste*
Skimmed milk	*Added to paste and hookbaits or mixed into groundbait for a cloud effect*
Eggs	*The white of egg (albumen) is used as a binding agent in carp and other paste hookbaits*

Above *Packed with high protein, trout pellets can be ground down to crumb size, then mixed with white of egg and lightly boiled to make a special carp bait.* Below *Seed hookbaits: top left, sweetcorn; right, hemp; bottom left, brown tares; right, stewed wheat.*

The carp angler has gone beyond using additives to attract fish. Part of his plans have been to concoct high-protein baits that have pulling power as well as the ability to stay on the hook when cast long distances. These baits are a mixture of high value food and glutinous material. The simplest must be ground trout pellets, the kind that can be bought from most tackle dealers and aquarists, mixed with white of egg. Other far more complicated recipes have been published by the carp lads. Most of the high protein hookbaits use PYM (Phillips yeast mixture); Casilan, which is a health food derived from milk, and Beemax, a wheat germ protein together with a bonding agent, such as eggs. The proportions are simple:

PYM	2 oz (56 g)
Casilan	1 oz (28 g)
Beemax	4 oz (113 g)

The powders are mixed together thoroughly before the white of three eggs is beaten in. The mixture should have a reasonably stiff texture. A pan of water is boiled and balls of the bait, about the size of a 10p piece, are dropped into the water. Boiling for just two minutes builds a tough outer skin onto each ball of bait. This helps to keep the bait on the hook during the cast, as well as providing a barrier to the feeding activities of small fry. They are prevented from worrying the bait to pieces before the bait is found by a carp.

The additive business doesn't end there for within the basic mixture one can add meat extract, either as Marmite or dog food, or as a mess of pounded-up casters and maggots. They are, after all, of high protein value. Recently while tench and carp fishing, I've had good results with the dry cat-food biscuits Munchies which are, according to the manufacturers, a blend of cereals, meat extracts, animal fat, wheat germ, dried yeast and colouring. For close-in fishing I use the whole biscuit slightly moistened, but longer casts need the Munchies to be pulverised to form a powder from which a moulded ball can be formed.

Casting high-protein paste bait over long distances can be difficult. It can be made easy by freezing the balls with the hooks already inserted. Freezing makes no difference to the quality of the bait, which quickly thaws out in water. The great advantage of freezing is that it will not fly off the hook even when belted out to 60 yards (55 m) or more.

Seed baits

Fish expect to find some seeds which have drifted down onto the water, carried by the wind. This does not happen all the year round. Late summer into autumn is the time when most plants drop their seeds and

HOOKING A SINGLE WHEAT GRAIN

Left *How to hook a single grain of wheat*. Above *Stew hempseed in an old saucepan (to avoid domestic friction) until the outer, black kernel splits to reveal the white seed*. Right *Three variations in hooking single hempseed grains*.

grains. Four seed baits have found favour with the coarse angler: wheat, tares, hemp and sweetcorn. Each of these seed baits can be bought as dried grains, prepared hookbaits with some form of preservative, or, in the case of sweetcorn, as a tinned food. Hempseed can also be obtained as a finely ground dust to be added to groundbait. It has a strong attraction for roach and chub and is worth using in conjunction with hemp hookbait.

Wheat

On a size 14 hook, individual wheat grains are a super trotting bait. After overnight soaking, the grains should be stewed for as long as it takes to produce a softish grain that has split slightly, showing the white of the inside. Wash the boiled grains in clean water, it will stop them sticking together. The same seeds can be loose fed, just a few grains at a time, to get the fish's interest. A light cloudbait mixture, into which a handful of wheat is added, makes a perfect, visible attractor to waiting fish.

Hemp

This bait has the reputation of bringing fish to a suicidal feeding frenzy. It is a slightly exaggerated reputation, but hempseed certainly has a powerful effect on roach, dace, chub and even barbel. It is primarily a

HEMPSEED

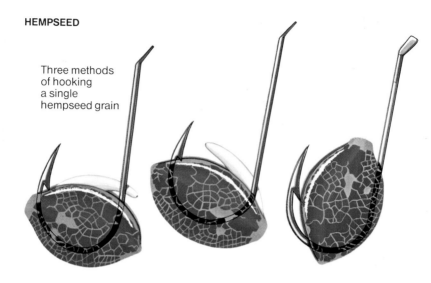

Three methods of hooking a single hempseed grain

trotting bait, yet there are times when I have resorted to hemping in stillwater. Hempseed has to be prepared for fishing. When bought it consists of extremely hard, black seeds resembling a No. 1 split shot. The seeds are boiled in an *old* saucepan until the outer, black skin splits, showing a bright, internal pith. Clean the hemp and cool it quickly by washing under a running tap.

Hempseed is very cheap. A pint is far more than one could use in a day's fishing and that includes its use as a loosefeed. Many anglers make the mistake of taking too much hempseed on an outing, overfeed the swim and complain that the fish aren't taking the bait. They then throw the excess seed into the river to complain on later outings that the fish will take no other bait! It is all a question of conditioning. Roach are one species that become addicted to hemp—not in the narcotic sense of course!

Fish hemp on a fine wire hook, a size 18 for a single grain, inserting the hook through the body of the seed so that the point emerges from the split-open skin. As an alternative, the hook should be gently pushed through the split so that the bend rests against the inner side of the skin. This places the hempseed neatly on the hook bend. Because hemp looks like and is similar in colour to split shot, *false* bites can be experienced, caused by fish striking at the shot that sinks the float. This problem can be overcome by using Styl leads or wrapping soft lead wire around the line, stopped by a split shot. This gives enough weight to cock the float but looks nothing like the bait in shape or colour.

Tares

The tare is a member of the pea family and is a larger seed than hemp. It grows wild among cereal crops and is riddled out when wheat and barley are being dried. You'll find tares in pet shops as the food for pigeons. Brown or black in colour, the tare has become very popular among Midland anglers, particularly when accompanied by loosefeeding with hemp. Again it is a warm-weather bait suitable for most fish other than the predatory species. It also seems to attract a larger size of fish. Put tares on at least a 16 hook, with the bulk of the seed hanging on the hook bend. The point, down to the barb, should just emerge from the tare.

Sweetcorn

This is maize, harvested but not dried. The best sweetcorn is always the soft-centred grain with a slightly toughened skin. You can boil maize to produce a soft hookbait but it will probably go mushy. It's very difficult to judge the correct amount of cooking time that will give the right texture of bait. So it is easier to buy it in a tin or as a *manufactured*

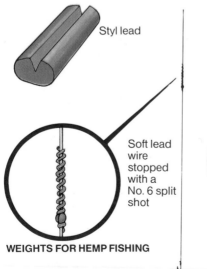

Styl lead

Soft lead wire stopped with a No. 6 split shot

WEIGHTS FOR HEMP FISHING

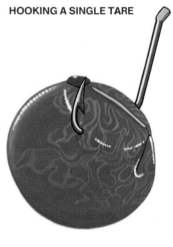

HOOKING A SINGLE TARE

hookbait. The kernels can be fished singly or as a multi-bait, on a size 14–10 gilt hook. It is a bait taken by carp, which means using a larger iron of stouter wire. I like sweetcorn as a legered bait. Certainly I have had more success with it as a static bait than any of the previously mentioned seedbaits, which have a trotting usage. Sweetcorn should be loosefed with half a dozen particles at intervals of a few minutes.

Ready-prepared seedbaits

Each of the four main seedbaits—wheat, tares, sweetcorn and hemp— can be bought preserved, but the chemicals used need to be completely washed out from the bait before fishing. Do this under a tap, because any preservative remaining will carry a detectable taint that discourages fish from feeding. Removal of smell is most important when using a static

Far left How to avoid the nuisance of fish biting at split shot when using hemp as bait. The cleverly designed Styl leads, or soft lead wire wrapped round the line, will cock the float. Left The way in which a tare should be hooked. Below Sweetcorn can be used either as a multi-bait or a single grain. With corn a gilt hook should be used, balanced to the size of the bait. Below right An elderberry should sit neatly on the hook-bend so as not to fall away when being cast. Preserved elderberries stay well on the hook.

HOOKING ELDERBERRY

HOOKING SWEETCORN

Three kernels on a No. 10 gilt hook

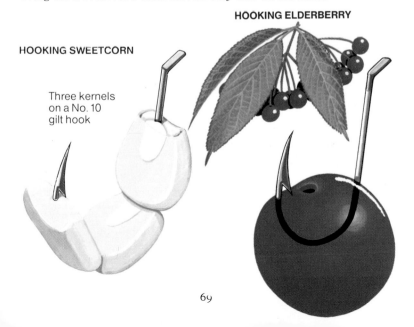

bait. Although fish mouth a bait, their sense of smell is more acute than that of taste. Smell, therefore, is important.

Fruits and berries

At one time or another, fish will take a dropping fruit. Like seeds, the natural process is for berries to fall in the autumn. I cannot vouch for their value as bait as, with the exception of the elderberry, I've never had much confidence in them. Ripe berries have always appeared too soft to put on the hook. They cannot be made ready beforehand like seeds. The elderberry resembles a hempseed, perhaps slightly larger but of the same coloration. Chub and roach will take them fished on a 16 hook, as a trotted bait.

Miscellaneous baits

There are a multitude of baits, some natural and others the product of the kitchen, that will take coarse fish. Potatoes are a carp bait that enjoyed enormous success some years ago. The potatoes were par-boiled, then threaded onto the hook link with a darning needle. Carp have to be conditioned to take such baits but once suspicious, perhaps after being caught, they soon avoid the offerings. Whole beans of the haricot, soya and broad varieties will be taken by carp although I think they can only be described as change baits that may be right for the odd occasion. I certainly would not use them as a first-choice bait. If you fancy experimenting with bean baits, remember to cook them first, as in the dried state they are too hard to put onto a hook and certainly not palatable to any fish. One thing in their favour is that these beans are easily seen by fish searching over the bottom for natural food.

Crustaceans and molluscs

There was a time when catching freshwater crayfish was a vital preliminary to winter chub fishing. Found in clean, running water, they are fairly easy to catch if their feeding habit is understood. Crayfish exist by eating the dead of other species. If a fillet of roach or even a lash of herring is placed into a drop net which is then lowered to the bed of a suitable stream, crayfish will soon scent the bait. Late evening is the best time to go about catching the bait. Keep them alive in a bucket of water.

To mount the crayfish, pass the point of a size 8–10 hook between the separated plates that cover the tail. Fish the bait on a free-line in shallow, running water, or on a light paternoster rig into the holes that undercut the high-sided banks of a meandering river. It is a form of highly mobile fishing, the angler moving down river to cover all the likely chub holes. The roving fisherman in winter keeps warm too!

Freshwater shrimps are not as big as their saltwater cousins. The tiny fellows will be taken by chub, roach and dace. Catch them with a fine meshed net in fast-running water that spills over dace shallows. They are only big enough to mount on a small hook, about size 18, but the shrimp can be useful when pleasure fishing on small streams.

Fish, the growing fry in particular, eat snails, mussels and freshwater limpets during their juvenile lives. Many of our largest freshwater species, notably the carp and bream, continue this feeding behaviour throughout their lives. The empty shells of swan mussels and water snails often litter the shallows. Very few fish are ever hooked on snails, whether they be ramshorn, pond or bladder species but a modicum of success can be had using the swan mussel as a hookbait.

Search for swan mussels in the shallow muddy waters of lakes and slow-running rivers. They can be raked out of the mud with a garden rake or by careful scraping with a landing net to dislodge them from the bottom. I keep them alive by taking them home to introduce them to a captive existence in my breeding pond. Although there is no mud, the mussels live happily until they finish their days on a hook. Unfortunately I lose a few to a largish tench, which can open the shells when I'm never there to see it done.

Opening mussels can be a hassle. A suitable knife is needed. Not a sharp one but something with a stout blade. Sea anglers use a similar knife to open the many kinds of shellfish used in salt water. The muscle, or hinge holding the two halves of shell, has to be cut. Don't ram the blade into the shell. You will either break the blade, smash up the flesh or both. Once cut, the hinge will relax allowing you to scrape out the contents. The mussel foot, with its bright orange, tough flesh, is the best bait. Use up the other scraps as an addition to your groundbait. A size 6–8 hook will give a balance between iron size and bait.

Below *Swan mussel is a good tench bait.* Below right *A knife for extracting shellfish should be rounded and near-blunt.*

MEAT BAITS

Meat, in two main forms, has become a prized bait by coarse anglers. Luncheon meat is probably the most popular among barbel and chub fishermen, and is the reason for the number of empty tins that are discarded at the waterside by thoughtless anglers. Quite rightly the farming community and some angling federations instantly ban anybody guilty of such vandalism. Having made the decision to fish with this bait, the proper way to carry it to the river is out of the tin, wrapped in a polythene bag to prevent the meat drying out. The same bag can be used to carry all other litter back home to the dustbin.

Luncheon meat is a convenient bait, easily cut into bait-sized cubes. In use, the two difficulties are in keeping it on the hook during the cast and then preventing fish from tearing it off the hook too easily. The answer is to insert a blade of grass, or similar material, across the hook bend. This prevents the slightly greasy meat from pulling off, particularly if the grass is flat against the meat with the central spine providing some rigidity.

Select the correct hook size by balancing the amount of luncheon meat so that the hook eye is only fractionally clear of the upper surface of the cube. I usually cut portions of about thumbnail size. These match a No. 8 round bend hook perfectly, with only a glimpse of hook bend and eye showing outside the bait. Luncheon meat has a pretty strong smell, which makes it both an attractive hookbait and one which can be used as loosefeed. Smaller pieces of the bait can be added to a stiff groundbait to give more volume and enhance the pulling power of the hookbait. Occasionally, I fish meat on the hook in conjunction with a swimfeeder filled with meat and crumb particles. The feed lies in close proximity to the hook and doesn't get dispersed so quickly by a strong current.

Sausage meat

Almost as good as luncheon meat and possibly cheaper to use, sausages have one drawback—the skins. Plastic skins, which all sausages seem to have these days, appear to deter fish from taking the bait. This is a pity, because the skin helps to keep the soft content on the hook. The answer is to buy plain sausage meat that can be stiffened up by the addition of some fine groundbait. This mixture produces a paste that can be moulded to the hook. Some anglers cook their sausage, or rather they boil it. This gets rid of excess fat but it is doubtful whether this gives any fishing advantage.

At various times, all manner of unusual meat baits have been known to take fish. An angler, in desperation putting on a piece of ham from his

A slip of grass placed between the luncheon meat square and the hook bend will prevent this soft bait flying off as the cast is made.

sandwich, may find it attracts a big chub; liver sausage, too, has taken fish. In areas such as the Norfolk Broads, where boating holidaymakers unwisely throw their kitchen rubbish overboard, fish can acquire a liking for bacon scraps. Anglers have found that inch-squares of the green kind, raw or cooked, and mounted on a No. 10 hook, have caught chub. But luncheon meat is the cheapest and most effective form of meat available to anglers.

Cheese baits

Cheese is a good chub bait throughout the fishing season. It can be used in cubes, rather like luncheon meat, or made into a paste. Many anglers have sung the praises of various kinds of cheese. Some prefer the smelly varieties and others the glutinous properties of the foil-covered, processed cheeses. What is vitally important is the texture of the chosen cheese. It *must* be soft. Something similar to a tacky breadpaste is desirable. An unfortunate property of cheese is that it goes hard when it enters cold water. At most times of the British fishing season, the temperature of the water is considerably cooler than that of the air. What appears to be a bait with perfect softness on the riverbank soon becomes a rock-hard morsel after lying on the bottom for a few minutes. Two things result from this: the fish are easily put off by a bait that is too hard, and striking with hardened cheese on the hook can be almost impossible.

For these reasons I adopt a policy of using cheese-paste made of one part cheese to two parts breadpaste. This doesn't harden to the same extent as cheese on its own. The bread content is unimportant and its use is only to carry the cheese flavouring down to the fish. Used as paste, cheese can be offered on a variety of hook sizes suited to other species. For example, roach will take tiny pieces mounted on hooks down to 18. For chub, a larger hook will be needed to match its larger mouth and huge appetite for sizeable baits. With cheese on the hook, groundbait with medium feed that has an addition of cheese to match the hook offering.

For fishing a livebait in stillwater use one of the great classic tackle items, the Jardine snaptackle.

FISH ON JARDINE SNAP-TACKLE FOR STILLWATER

Using fish baits

Although most coarse fish will take livebaits at some time in their lives, we tend to think of fish as baits for predators. Pike, zander and perch are the obvious species but there are others. The brown trout is a serious predator in rivers and streams and the eel must not be discounted. Even the chub, which most people associate with taking standard trotted or legered baits, can be lured with a fish livebait. Deadbaits will prove deadly to pike and large eels, both species naturally feeding on carrion, scavenging the dead and sick members of various shoal fish.

Livebaiting for pike

Pike are territorial fish, which means that they live and feed in well-established areas that suit their lifestyle. Unlike the zander, pike tend to select places to lie offering clean water which is also clear of mud and other suspended material that would spoil their vision. The pike has eyes which face forward, giving perfect binocular vision. In other words, pike hunt by sight.

Ideally, a livebait should be presented where it can be seen easily.

This method of attaching a livebait to terminal tackle is effective when fishing in running water, for it keeps the bait lively.

■SH ON JARDINE SNAP-TACKLE FOR RUNNING WATER

That generally means suspending the bait below a float, and slightly above the pike's natural lie. From where it lies, the pike can see the bait at some distance, silhouetted against the skylight. In 4 ft (1.2 m) of water, set the bait at about 2–3 ft (0.5–1 m) below the float. Use a bait full of life, for its movements are the main attraction to any predator. Make sure that the terminal live-bait rig does not kill or hamper the movements of the fish.

The float does two things: it suspends the bait at a given depth but, more importantly, it gives an indication of what the bait is doing. Each motion of the float will tell the watching fisherman what is happening below the surface of the water. How you mount the bait is vital. Take a snap tackle and set the gap between the trebles to match the size of the baitfish. The ideal setting is for the end treble hook to be inserted, by one point only, into the side of the bait's mouth. The other treble, which can be moved along the wire trace to accommodate any size of fish, is fixed below the leading edge of the bait's dorsal fin. This method suits fishing

On the previous pages, methods are shown of hooking livebait when fishing in still and running water. Here is a further method using a rig with only a single hook and a treble. This rig is for running water.

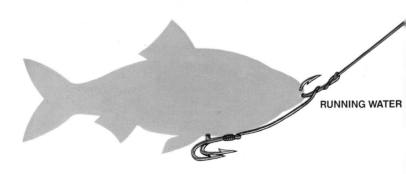

RUNNING WATER

a livebait in stillwaters or in rivers that lack any marked current pull. When faced with running water, the rig must be altered markedly by fixing the rear treble into the tissue below the dorsal fin. The adjustable treble is nicked into the bony mouth of the bait. This set-up allows the fish to swim against the current in a natural fashion and ensures that the bait is not dragged sideways against the flow when it is being reeled in. Water entering the gills instead of through the mouth will soon injure the fish and it will no longer be a useful bait.

These two live-baiting methods can be fished using a shop-bought Jardine snap tackle. Some anglers (and I am one of them), prefer to use a simpler rig based on one treble and a large single hook. In stillwater, the single hook is used to suspend the bait by passing it through the thick tissue just under the dorsal fin, the treble is fixed, one point only, through the bony jaw. In rivers and streams the single is passed through the upper jaw of the fish, with the treble nicked into the skin in front of the anal fins.

Another live-bait rig, for use in still water. The single hook passes through the muscle tissue just below the dorsal, while one point of the treble is passed through the jaw bone.

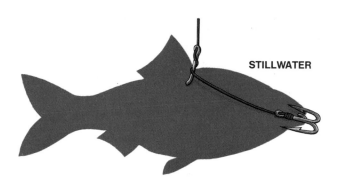

STILLWATER

Because they are lively and because of their coloration, roach make the best livebaits for pike. They can be easily seen by a feeding pike. Small bream can be used, although I have not had any significant success with them. For big pike, such as the monsters reputed to inhabit many of our larger lakes, a sizeable perch or even a jack pike might be the meal required to lure the larger fish. Jack pike between 3 and 5 lb have been used occasionally with success. The tackle remains the same, but the size of hooks and strength of line must be upgraded to cope with large livebait.

For most pike fishing I use size 4 trebles in company with No. 2 single hooks. The snap tackles are made from single-strand Alasticum wire of 14 lb (6 kg) b.s. which has certain anti-kink properties and doesn't rust. However, it is false economy to keep traces after hard usage. Dismantle the rig and replace the wire after each fishing session.

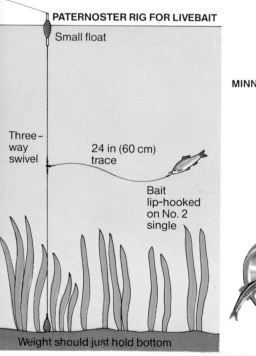

PATERNOSTER RIG FOR LIVEBAIT

Small float

Three-way swivel

24 in (60 cm) trace

Bait lip-hooked on No. 2 single

Weight should just hold bottom

MINNOW TRAP

Current flow

Livebaiting for zander

This fish has a different life style to that of the pike. This foreign intruder, now well-established in British waters, lives happily in muddy conditions and appears to favour slow or still waters. The species hunts in packs, moving through a water to find food rather than adopting the static, territorial behaviour of pike. Zander, also called pike-perch, will take small roach, dace and minnow baits. Mount them on a paternostered rig. I prefer the paternoster for it gives immediate warning of excited movement from the bait. The float should be of the lightest possible but use sufficient weight to keep the float holding against any slight flow. Zander have a habit of dropping any bait which their senses feel has an unnatural appearance or offers too much resistance to their attack. So the bait must be able to move freely on the nylon trace.

Far left The paternoster livebait rig can be adapted for use with a variety of baitfish for perch, zander and pike. Left An easily constructed minnow trap. Tap the concave centre out of the base of a wine bottle and support it as shown. Below A simplified deadbait rig for mounting herring or mackerel, it can be adapted to take any other suitable species and size of freshwater fish.

DEADBAIT TACKLE

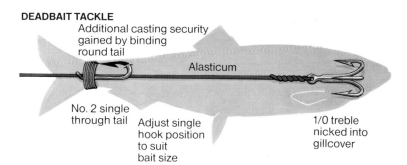

Additional casting security gained by binding round tail

Alasticum

No. 2 single through tail

Adjust single hook position to suit bait size

1/0 treble nicked into gillcover

Minnows can be caught on very fine float tackle when livebaits are needed but time can be saved by trapping them. Build your own by knocking out the concave centre of a wine bottle. Stretch a scrap of muslin net over the neck of the bottle and tie it securely with a long piece of string, which will also act as the means of lowering it into the stream. Search for minnows in crystal clear water where it runs over gravel shallows. Stuff some bread flake or white groundbait into the bottle. Lower the bottle into the stream with the closed neck upstream. Leave it tethered there and await the arrival of the tiny fish. They swim into the bottle but cannot all escape when the bottle is lifted, due to the concave shape of the base. Transfer the minnows to a white polythene can where they can be seen when you need a bait.

One of the traditional methods of winter fishing, the sink-and-draw style is based on a moving bait and a mobile angler. It reproduces the erratic, jerky movements of a sick or injured fish.

THE SINK-AND-DRAW STYLE

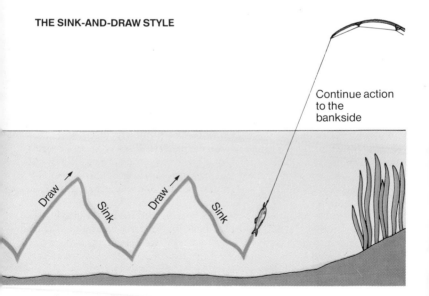

Continue action
to the
bankside

Draw Sink Draw Sink

DEADBAIT MOUNT FOR SINK-AND-DRAW STYLE

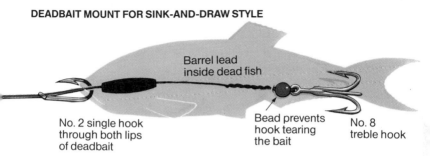

Barrel lead
inside dead fish

No. 2 single hook
through both lips
of deadbait

Bead prevents
hook tearing
the bait

No. 8
treble hook

The simple mounting of a deadbait for sink-and-draw style fishing.
Here, minnows and other small, shiny cyprinids are ideal.

Deadbaiting for pike

This is a technique that has produced some massive fish. Perhaps the
larger pike are slow in their movements and have different feeding habits
to those of the smaller fish. Big pike rarely chase spinners but they do
need to feed regularly. A dead fish, lying where they can see it, must
arouse the big pike. I must emphasize that to be successful a deadbait,
like a live bait, needs to be seen. Although pike undoubtedly find some
food by sense of smell, most of their hunting is concerned with vision. It
is no use casting a deadbait out to lie deep within a thick layer of bottom
weed. Such a bait must rest on a clean river or lake beds.

Most of the coarse fish species will make perfectly acceptable dead
baits. However, deadbaiting relies on the predators' scavenging instincts
so we can use sea fish. Herrings, mackerel and sprats are easily bought
and can be stored in the freezer until required. I use one rig for deadbait.
Again, it is constructed of Alasticum wire with one treble, size 1/0, and a
No. 2 single hook.

Fix the treble into the gillcover of a herring and insert the single into
the root of the bait's tail. Additional casting security can be gained by
tying the wire against the body, at the tail, with elasticated thread. I
don't use more than two hooks, for if the initial take of the feeding pike is
not recognized the fish may swallow the hooks. Nobody wants to kill fish
unnecessarily, so the minimum of hooks coupled with constant attention

to the line or bite indicator helps to minimise that possibility. A pike finding a deadbait has plenty of time to take the bait. The pike's movement over a considerable length of nylon between angler and bait may be hardly detectable. For this reason, some anglers advocate the use of a float when deadbaiting so that they can be alerted quickly to underwater events concerning the bait.

Sink and draw tactics

This is a superb method for taking pike, with the bonus of zander in the correct waters. The sink-and-draw technique depends on mobility, both of the angler and his bait. The bait is constantly cast into likely pike lies, then retrieved in a manner that suggests the erratic actions of a sick fish. By raising the rod top, the bait is drawn up through the water, then the rod is lowered while a small amount of line is reeled in. This lets the bait sink, wobbling through the depths. The whole sequence is repeated, the bait being cast and retrieved constantly back to the angler's pitch.

The rig is simple: a length of wire, two hooks, a bead and a barrel lead. The treble is fixed to the wire with a bead slipped on next to the hook eye to prevent the trace pulling through the fish. Then, with a baiting needle, the wire is passed through the length of the fish until it emerges from the bait's mouth. Fix the single hook so that it effectively seals both lips of the bait, after slipping a barrel lead down inside the throat. Finish off the trace with a barrel swivel.

The same system can be adapted to fishing with a minnow for perch, although there is no need to use wire in this rig. Alternatively, the minnow can be mounted on a spinning flight, available from tackle dealers, which incorporates sufficient weight to cast and sink the bait as well as imparting a spinning action via the plastic vanes. Minnows are a running-water species and as a spun bait are best used in a river or stream by being cast across at an angle of 45 degrees, to allow the current to work the bait across the flow. As they lie among the weedbeds, pike will see the arrival of the spun minnow as a flash of silver above their heads. This form of bait presentation puts a lot of line twist onto the reel even if a barrel swivel is used, so add an anti-kink device.

Top right A spinning mount for fishing with a dead minnow. The needle is inserted into the fish through the mouth. One prong of the treble hooks pierces each flank of the fish. Casting weight is carried on the mount. Right Blade spinners reproduce the disturbance in water made by a fleeing fish. This lure is most effective when cast across the current or retrieved fairly quickly to create the actions of a live fish.

HOW THE BLADE SPINNER WORKS

The blade revolves round a
fixed spindle on a
free-running saddle,
giving a vigorous
impression of
a fleeing fish

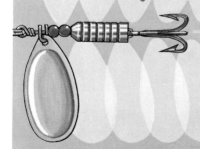

Spinning with artificial lures

Spinning can be a highly successful fishing style for the freshwater predatory species. The ideal lure (or bait as they are sometimes called), should have a good action that represents the natural or flight patterns of fish. Some colour is important for, seen as momentary flashes, it aids representation. Gold and red will give a lure the appearance of the rudd, one of the pike's favourite meals. The lure must have enough weight to cast easily and a shape that does not mask the hooks. Additional life or action is put into the lure by the angler. The way in which a lure is retrieved is vital. Spinning isn't a matter of casting and reeling in.

Among the many patterns of blade or bar spinners is the Colorado. A few years ago it was used extensively by pike anglers, many times with marked success. This heavy spinner needs to be worked fairly fast in order to create the disturbance and vibrations of a fast-swimming fish. A pike's head carries sensory pores which recognize the variations in water pressure heralding the presence of an erratically swimming fish. These indications, coupled with the pike's keen binocular vision, allow the predator to home-in on its prey. Sink-and-draw style can also be used with the blade spinner.

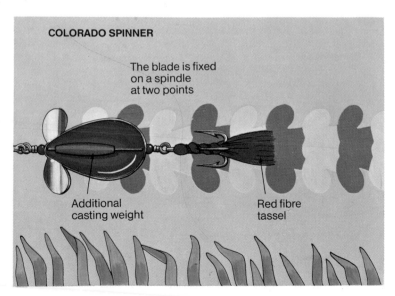

COLORADO SPINNER

The blade is fixed
on a spindle
at two points

Additional
casting weight

Red fibre
tassel

Thought and careful selection of the water to be covered is vital. The spinning lures roughly divide into three groups:

Those that truly spin
Lures that wobble or swerve
Plugs that have a variety of motion

The first category, spinners, have a metal blade revolving around a fixed bar which carries the treble hook and a weighted body. The blade spinner spins rapidly, either by the flow of current when used in a river, or by the forward movement when the angler reels the lure back. These lures are efficient, but notorious for putting twist into the reel line. This evil can be cured by placing an anti-kink vane above a swivel joining the reel line to the spinning trace. For trout or perch spinning, the trace need only be of nylon but a wire trace at least 6 in (15 cm) long is necessary for pike fishing.

Some kinds of blade spinners have fluted edges to the blades, said to create added turbulence or vibrations in the water. They are also highly colourful, which doesn't detract from the spinners' usefulness. A choice of colours helps to match the bait fish that is being simulated and vivid flashes from red spots or stripes look something like the flared gills of a distressed fish.

The blade spinner can be cast across the current, letting the current pressure swing the spinner round in an arc toward the angler's bank. Depth is adjusted by adding a Wye or spiral lead above the barrel swivel. In stillwaters, the action is put into the lure by the angler. Rate of retrieve will establish both the speed and the motion that the lure displays. It is a good idea to fish the spinner in a *sink-and-draw* fashion, winding erratically to add life to the lure.

Spoons

The spoon wobbles invitingly through the water because the maker has stamped a particular bend into the bar of metal. The degree of bend, coupled with the size of the lure and its weight, are essential components of a good spoon. Casting weight can vary considerably without any increase in the size of the spoon, only the thickness changes. I do not recommend the addition of weight above the lure. Spoons have the action built in, which means that any additional weight ahead on the trace will only dampen the action down, and that is the last thing wanted.

There are many colour patterns offered among the spoons currently in use around the world. Many of the colour shapes denote particular manufacturers' products. No doubt, some of the gaudiness is intended

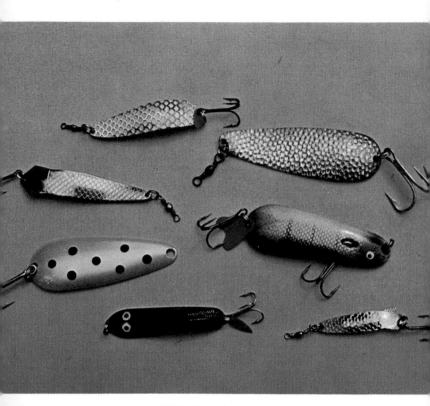

to make them attractive to fishermen rather than a serious effort at duplicating natural creatures. But the action is what matters. If colour becomes important, it is in the general, all-over sense. The copper spoon, often seen with a flash of red paint, is a favourite among pike men. Given a slow, undulating retrieve the spoon does look something like a wounded rudd.

Colour has historical importance in spinning. Spring fishing produced silver and blue lures as right for the season, whereas autumn suggested brown and gold, or red and gold. The base colours are easy to attain, because of the natural colour of brass, copper and chromium plate. But it often happens that one is forced to use a dirty, battered old spoon from the bottom of the tackle box—and that spoon catches. Why?

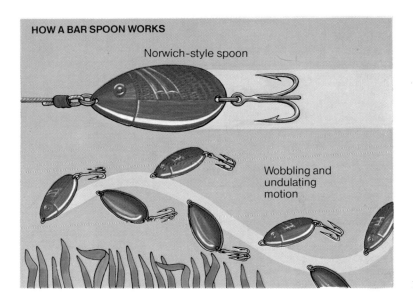

HOW A BAR SPOON WORKS

Norwich-style spoon

Wobbling and
undulating
motion

Above *The bar spoon has an undulating action that closely resembles the flight behaviour of a wounded shoalfish. A flash of red on a copper spoon may suggest a rudd to a feeding predator.*
Left *A group of spoon lures:* top, *Japanese wobbler;* 2nd row, left, *Shanny spoon;* 2nd row, right, *Broadland Specimen;* 3rd row, left, *Polkadot spoon;* 3rd row, right, *Frog wobbler;* bottom row, left, *Caterpillar spoon;* bottom row, right, *Toby spoon.*

Because newness and colour do not matter, what *does* is action and speed of retrieve.

The spoon can be fished in both still and running water, though I have a fancy that spoons have the edge in rivers and streams when worked by the prevailing current. The subtleties of the stream, little eddies and riffles, each produce a working pressure on the spoon that no amount of exaggerated winding in could possibly attain. If there is one golden rule, it is to spin slow and deep in winter, increasing in speed during the warmer months to match the predator's habit of rising up in the water to follow the prey. When pike fishing especially, a slow and steady retrieve of the line is vital. Pike stalk their prey and can be put off by any jerky movements of a lure.

Plugs: baits of wood and plastic

Our fishing cousins in America are responsible for the plug. Again, they are all about action. Being made of light material, many plugs float. The heavier wooden ones sink. These two properties, combined with the fitting of a forward vane, determine whether the plug fishes sub-surface or dives down deep when retrieved. Most deep-diving plugs are made from floating material. This ensures that a diver can be effectively fished across the lakebed while the reel handle is being turned. As soon as the handle stops turning, forward momentum ceases and the plug floats to the top of the water.

Plugs are made in some weird shapes. With the possible exception of the Rapala and its copies they do not look like anything that swims. But don't be put off by the peculiar design of many plug baits. Most of them

Right *All these lures are part of the pike angler's armoury of surface-running and deep-diving plugs. They come in a multitude of sizes, shapes, colours and can be manufactured from wood, plastic or metal.* **Below** *Apart from the surface-fished patterns, other plugs have an adjustable or pre-set vane which establishes the angle and depth to which the plug will dive.*

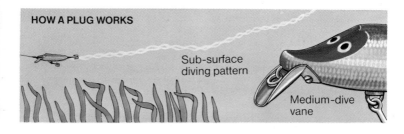

HOW A PLUG WORKS

Sub-surface diving pattern

Medium-dive vane

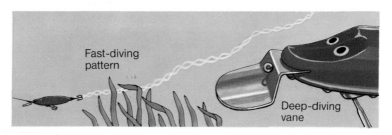

Fast-diving pattern

Deep-diving vane

work extremely well. The plug fisherman should acquire a collection offering the various actions needed for this branch of angling. They are:

Divers	Deep divers
Surface plugs	Audio plugs
Fast wigglers	Slow wigglers

Of these, the surface plugs are most effective in waters where there is a thick growth of bottom weed; even the tangling fronds that reach near to

Some plugs are described as 'sonic'. As they waggle through the water they create vibrations which travel as sound waves. The theory is that pike will be attracted to the vibrations.

the surface can be fished through. The audio plug has a small bead inside the hollow plug body. The bead is supposed to rattle with the vigorous motion of the plug. Whether this actually attracts feeding predators I cannot say, having never had an offer from a pike when using this type of bait.

The various wiggles given by different patterns of plug do have an attraction to fish. The fast, swerving action of small plugs (some are made in the Far East), has brought a fair number of smallish pike to

Many plugs are articulated, some with two parts, a few others with three. The parts are joined by a free-swinging junction which allows the plug to waggle attractively as it is slowly retrieved.

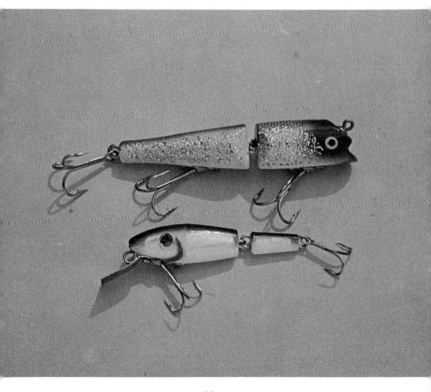

around the 5–8 lb (2.2–3.5 kg) mark. It is with the slow-actioned plugs that I have had my greatest plugging moments. The articulated plugs, where the elongated body is joined by a metal bar, have that swervy movement that appeals to me and, as I've found, to larger fish.

Fred Buller, a great pike man and author of many books concerned with big fish, suggested many years ago that anglers could vastly improve the action of their lures by the manner in which they were mounted on the trace. Fred advises using a stiff wire trace, about 5 in (127 mm) long with a 2 in (51 mm) diameter loop formed at the connection with the plug. The plug is free to swerve backwards and forwards around the loop, increasing its mobility. Fred says that a tight connection, such as a snap link on a normal wire trace, inhibits the plug's in-built movement.

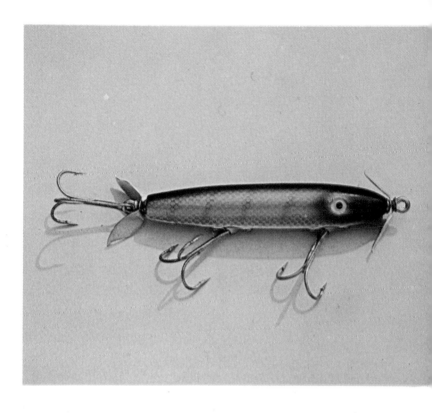

Above *This surface plug carries propellors that create a wake as the lure is drawn across the top of the water. It imitates a swimming animal such as the water-vole.* Left *Fred Buller's adaptation of a wire plug trace that allows greater action to be produced by the lure.*

There are many lures that have the addition of propellers at the front, back or both ends of the plug body. I don't like them although I have had some small success with pike using them in Denmark on a large lake. The pike fairly tore in to the plugs as they worked a little under the surface. The plugs lack diving vanes, relying on their weight to send them down in the water.

TREBLE-HOOK SIZE CHART

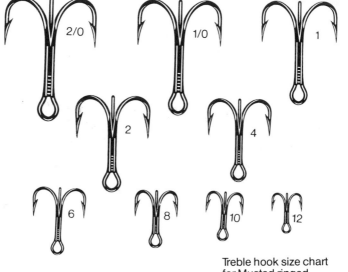

Treble hook size chart
for Mustad ringed,
short-shank pattern 3591A

Hooks for artificial lures

As I have written in a previous page, most plugs, spinners and spoons have a good action. Even the cheap, imported ones are reliable, simply because they are accurate copies of proven lures from America and Europe. Where some of them suffer is in the quality and size of the hooks mounted on the lures. Some hooks are far too rank in the barb and thick in the wire. There are also lures that have hooks too small to be effective.

Changing the hook size on a lure has to be done with great care as some kinds are remarkably touchy, the hook number—treble, double or single—and size have a considerable effect on the way in which the lure works. I once decided to change two treble hooks to singles on a Rapala-type lure that I have caught a lot of fish with. I made certain that the two replacement singles were of the same weight as the original trebles, but the action of the plug was totally ruined. The lure just didn't perform with single hooks. Obviously, the shape and mass of the trebles was vital to the action that the plug was intended to give.

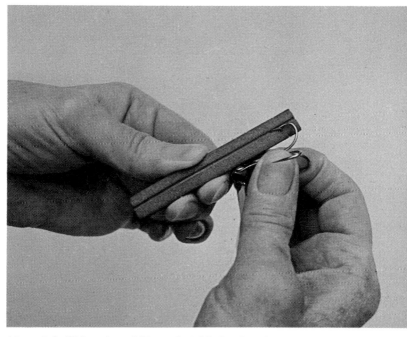

Above left *This range of Mustad treble hooks, shown correct size, runs through the large 2/0 down to size 12.* Above *Like most hooks, trebles are not always sharp enough when bought; nor do they retain their sharpness when kept in a box with other hooks and odd items of terminal tackle. Always carry a carborundum stone in your tackle box in order to give the hook points a sharpen before attaching them to the line. There is no excuse for losing a fish because your hook was not sharp enough. Never put wet hooks away with other dry ones unless you use stainless steel.*

Always ensure that the points on treble hooks are sharp. When bought, they rarely hook fish effectively. You only need buy a small, fine-grade carborundum stone. It is a welcome addition to any lure box. The other thing to guard against is letting artificial lures rattle around in boxes made of metal or hard plastic, for the hooks soon lose their fine points. Small cardboard boxes are the best containers.

The minnow

This lure is a frequently used spinning lure that falls between the plug and the blade spinner. The best minnows are made of wood or light plastic, like the plug, and yet they spin fast like a blade spinner. Devon minnow bodies have two transparent fins that spin around in the current. A stiff wire mount carries the swivel, for attachment, and a treble hook. Additional weight in the form of soft lead wire can be wrapped around the wire mount. Although originally used as a salmon spinning lure, I use small wooden minnows for perch and trout fishing in running water where they have a slight edge over metal lures because of their neutral buoyancy. Cast across the stream, the minnow will effectively swing round in mid-water.

Right Today's anglers can fish with lures such as these. When dapped on the surface of the water they represent live creatures. Below A classic lure, the Devon minnow is much favoured by salmon anglers. It can be obtained both as a metal lure with considerable weight and as a neutral-buoyancy, wooden midwater lure.

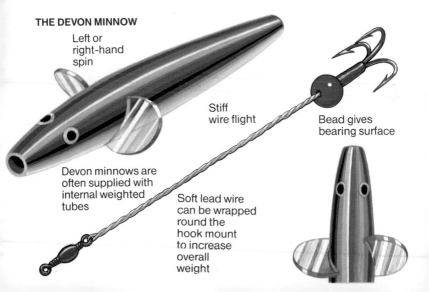

THE DEVON MINNOW

Left or right-hand spin

Stiff wire flight

Bead gives bearing surface

Devon minnows are often supplied with internal weighted tubes

Soft lead wire can be wrapped round the hook mount to increase overall weight

Miscellaneous lures

Take a look in most fishing tackle catalogues and you will find a few
dozen plastic replicas of frogs, beetles, worms and sundry other
creatures. They come from across the Atlantic where there are many
more predatory species than one finds in Europe. I know they work, for I
have used them in Canada. But there seemed always to be so many
hungry fish around that I am sure a twist of silver paper would have had
the same success! Apart from isolated lochans in the Highlands of
Scotland and in the West of Ireland, our waters are subjected to far
greater angling pressures than are experienced in the Americas. Our fish
tend to reject anything that looks, smells or behaves suspiciously.

Above *The rocky shore is a haven for a huge family of marine animals, many of which make useful baits. Try to inspect such a habitat at low-water in order to pin-point the various colonies of shellfish.* Below *Every kind of animal has its preferred area on a rocky shore. They seek quarters that suit their ability to withstand the non-stop, constant and unrelenting pounding of the waves and the regular pull of the tides.* Below right *The periwinkle, a shellfish that provides a tiny bait for small sea fish.*

THE BAIT-GATHERING ZONE ON A ROCKY SHORE

Splash zone
Periwinkles,
small and rough species

Average high-water mark

Broken ground –
Crab zone

Limpets Barnacles   Rockface

Mussels Common periwinkles

Shrimps Small fish

Rockpool

Low water (neap tide)

Low water (spring tide)

BAITS FOR SEA ANGLING

Sea anglers are fortunate when we consider their baits. Much of what catches fish can be gathered from the shore or within the littoral waters. Unlike the freshwater angler who buys maggots and bread in vast quantities, the sea angler need purchase very little. Collecting bait from the shoreline demands a complete understanding of the tidal phases, allied to the rise and fall for the section of coast most often visited. Bait is *always* there but there are times when it is inaccessible.

Bait from the rocky shore

Shellfish that adhere to the rocks below the high tide mark are the most available bait. Depending on the strength of the tide and power of the waves that strike upon the rocky coastline, bait will be found in a number of habitats. All but the strongest shellfish, such as limpets that can holdfast in a full gale, seek a home out of the main thrust of waves and tide. They fix themselves in the cracks that fissure most of the rock and cliff bases. The bait found is the natural food for the species of fish that inhabit this type of coastline. Apart from the small fry of rock fish species, there is little else of bait value to be gathered from the environment.

You should arrive at the fishing venue at the time of the lowest tide level possible, because some of the valuable bait forms live close to the low-water mark. They do not like being exposed by a dropping tide for too long. There are two reasons for this: without water, their ability to find food is impaired, and prolonged exposure to wind and sunlight soon kills them. The common periwinkle, though small, makes a bait for

small rockfish such as the wrasse and pollack. Two or three winkles on a hook have an enticing effect on fish as they exude a strong smell into the surrounding water. They are easily gathered because this small mollusc can tolerate long periods out of water. It is found living in the splash zone, higher up the shore than any other species. Deeper down the rock faces we find the limpet and acorn barnacle. Gouged out from its conical shell the former makes a good bait for wrasse. Freeing the limpet can defeat the newcomer to bait gathering. When left above the tideline by the receding water, the limpet raises its shell a fraction from the rock, and exudes mucus as a barrier against drying out. At this time the limpet has slightly relaxed its tight hold on the rockface. The secret is to give the limpet a sharp tap before it detects your presence on the rocks. It will fall away—if your approach has been stealthy enough. Limpets can be used whole or as cut pieces added to a small worm to form a cocktail bait. Pollack and rock codling find this combination to their liking.

The dog whelks tend to forage among the patches of barnacle spat. They aren't fond of direct light, so tend to be found in the darker crevices that are choked with immature barnacles and limpets. The whelks are a valuable hookbait for rock fishing. Try not to smash up the contents of any shell. Get the flesh from the shell by carefully cracking the whelk open with a fishing lead. Hook the whelk through the toughened foot where a secure hookhold can be had when using a fine wire iron. I like the smaller Aberdeen sizes for fishing with these baits.

Farther down the rock faces, very close to the mean low water mark, three more shellfish are found; the saddle oyster which attaches itself by the shell to any smooth area, a small scallop of the *Chlamys* species and the mussel. Of these baits, the mussel must stand out as the best. It has a unique method of attaching itself to any piece of rock, and colonies of mussels can be found formed around wooden or metal pilings. The mussel's foot secretes a mass of tough threads, called a *byssus*, by which it forms an attachment to the rough projections from which mussels cannot be removed without the application of considerable force.

Mussels can be used fresh after careful extraction from their shells. They are semi-liquid, and it is extremely difficult to get them to stay on a

Above right *Limpets are a useful wrasse and pollack bait. They can be used on the hook whole or as pieces tipped with a small worm.* Right *Dog whelks can be used as bait for the fish species that live near rocks, or for legering for flatfish. To get them from their shell, crack it without spoiling the creature, or dip it briefly into boiling water.* Far right *Mussels are found in huge colonies.*

hook, especially if one is long casting or fishing in rough seas. I get them out of the shells by using the same blunt knife as used on freshwater mussels (see page 71). Take care when opening a mussel shell, its extremely brittle and sharp edges can give a nasty cut. Many anglers boil the mussel for a couple of minutes to open the shells and toughen the body of the mollusc. In the past few years, wild mussels have gained the reputation of being responsible for food poisoning among humans. This is caused by the way in which the mussel feeds. It can tolerate high levels of pollution but gathers what can be toxic wastes within its tissues. Providing you don't eat them, there is no reason why they shouldn't be gathered for bait. Some enterprising fishermen are farming the mussel on rafts, set out in sea loughs in the West of Ireland, to provide supplies for restaurants.

Mussels are found in their millions on any rocky shore and can provide a year-round bait for the angler who is prepared to gather and shell the creature. It has a tremendous attraction for cod and haddock, although I do confess to adding a tippet of lugworm when beachfishing. If your mussels are too soft, tie them on by wrapping a bunch of the bait with some knitting wool.

Another filter feeder, found on the same rocky ledges as the mussel, is the acorn barnacle. It is hardly worth considering from a bait point of view, but is preyed on by both the dog whelk and chitons of which the former is also of angling interest.

Those are the bait creatures that attach themselves to rock. Other bait animals are actually found *inside* the rock. This may seem strange but

Above, far left *To aid casting a soft bait, the mussel can be tied onto the hook with wool.* Above left *Boiling mussels makes them tougher—ideal for staying on the hook.* Above *Mussel rafts in Killary Bay, Connemara. Strings of shellfish are grown on cords that hang in the pollution-free water.* Below *Acorn barnacles crowd the lower splash zone on any rocky shore. They make a small and hardly hookable bait for inshore fish species.*

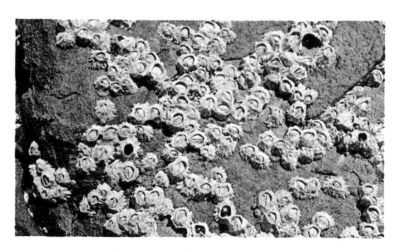

when we take a close look at the types of rock that form the sea cliffs and low rocky platforms of Britain and the western seaboard of the Atlantic Ocean, there is great variation in the composition of the strata. Each type of rock has its own particular collection of marine creatures, some clinging to the rock, others boring into it. Bait-seeking anglers will be interested in a bivalve mollusc known as the piddock. Looking something like a clam, this shellfish bores into sandstone and limestone cliffs. I don't suggest that we ought to tear limestone cliffs apart to find the piddock, only that a fall of broken chalk at the waterline may be worth your inspection!

The next place to consider as a bait-gathering zone is among the loose rock at the base of sea cliffs and around any rock peninsula that has a gentle wave action. This is a rich place for all manner of bait. You'll find most opportunity by turning the boulders and scrabbling among the weed fronds that blanket the stones. The shore crab is our immediate target and forms a very valuable bait for both shore and boat anglers. It is used in three stages of the crab's growth: as a 'peeler', 'softie' and 'crispie'. To understand these descriptions, let us take a look at the way in which crustaceans grow. They have no bone structure. The hard part of the crab is its body shell. As the crab gets bigger it has to shed the shell

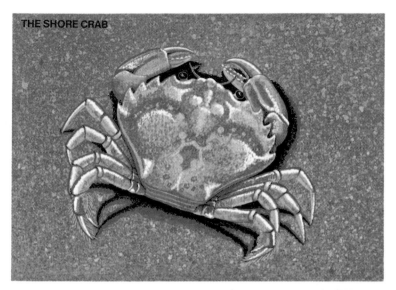

Above *The shore crab makes an effective bait in its peeler and soft forms, but must be carefully mounted on the hook.*
Left *On the lower areas of the rocky shore, where the water recedes only for an hour or so, crabs can be found in the pools among the thick weed growth and the clutter of loose water-rolled rocks. This kind of habitat also harbours all kinds of bait-sized molluscs, gastropods and crustaceans, and all can be used as bait.*
Right *A crab can only increase its size by producing a new shell larger than the old one. When the time comes to shed the old shell, it peels off (hence the name 'peeler crab') to reveal the new, larger, one already formed.*

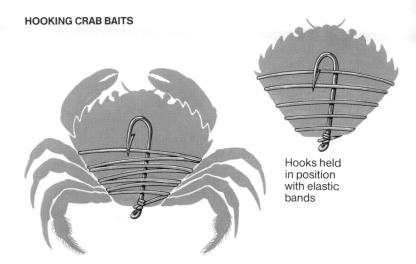

Hooks held
in position
with elastic
bands

to accommodate this growth. It has no other way to grow larger.

The crab seeks shelter as the time for shedding occurs, as it is then vulnerable to attack by fish. The hard shell begins to peel away, revealing the new, soft shell underneath. Although still hard, the outer shell can be easily prised away before the crab is used as a hookbait. Detection of the peeler stage is done by gently twisting one of the legs. In the peeler stage, the hard shell will come away revealing a soft, fleshy leg intact.

After discarding the old, hard shell, the soft-backed crab has to wait a while before the new shell hardens. This time is spent in growing fast. The softie makes a superb bait that will be taken by almost any species of fish. Bass anglers prize them above all else. Obviously, a soft crab has to be mounted on the hook with care. Too much force in casting will rip the bait clear of the hook. To overcome this problem, the bait should be held on the hook by an elastic band. The soft bait can also be stolen by the hardback crabs that abound on the seabed off most shores. Whole softies are especially easy to steal, the live crabs tearing at the legs until the bait is completely shredded. Take off the legs and claws, giving fish a mouthful that they can take quickly. The claws and legs can then be fished as a bunch after all the valuable body baits are used up.

This process of crabs and fish whittling a bait down to mouth size can happen when using crab bait for flounders. These fish are notorious for worrying a bait without actually taking the hook. Unless they are about the size of a 50p piece, use only whole crabs for bass and cod. Otherwise it is better to fish the softback in pieces. If fish tear the bait away, even when tied on to the hook with elastic bands or thread, try mounting the bait on a treble hook. Take the treble up through the bait's belly. The nylon is then tied on to the hook eye emerging from the back of the crab.

As its new shell hardens, the crab becomes known as a crispy. Squeezed between thumb and finger, the softness is still felt but there is a springiness about the shell. Mount this bait without piercing it with a hook, tying it on with elastic. The crab will then be free to roam around, tethered by the sinker, its activities attracting the fish.

Crabs can be kept for a limited period of time, but they must not be allowed to dry out. A wooden box, with a secure lid, into which a number of $\frac{1}{2}$ in (13 mm) diameter ventilation holes have been bored,

Left Crab baits can be held on the hook by elastic bands as well as wool. They prevent a soft-skinned peeler crab bait from flying off while being cast. Below Many baits can be found in rockpools.

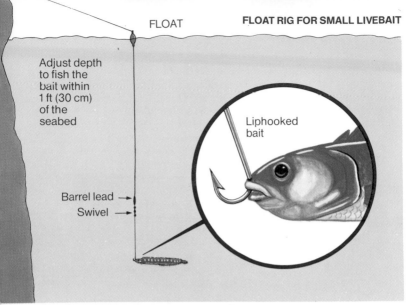

FLOAT RIG FOR SMALL LIVEBAIT

FLOAT

Adjust depth
to fish the
bait within
1 ft (30 cm)
of the
seabed

Liphooked
bait

Barrel lead
Swivel

BAIT-GATHERING ZONE ON SANDY SHORE

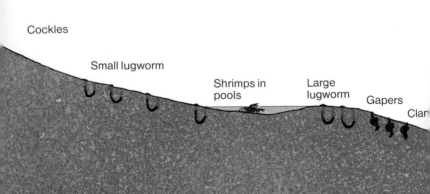

Cockles

Small lugworm

Shrimps in
pools

Large
lugworm

Gapers

Clar

containing wet seaweed provides both a storing and travelling habitat. The weed should be changed every day if possible.

Peeler crabs are found in the warmer months of the year and yet they can be at their most effective when the cod begin to appear at the beginning of November. I freeze crabs to ensure better winter catches. It can work if a few simple precautions are met. After removing the claws and legs, insert a cod-size hook into the body, taking the point in via a leg socket, which is a strong hookhold on an otherwise delicate bait. Stainless steel hooks obviate any rusting during the freezing process.

Wrap a packet of about ten crabs at a time in greaseproof paper or put them into sealable plastic bags. They need to be airtight, for if they aren't the crabs will dry out and become useless. I have found that crabs will keep frozen and in good condition for three months. Why insert the hooks at the freezing stage? The reason is that it is almost impossible to put a frozen bait onto a hook with cold hands in the middle of winter without smashing up the bait; and a frozen bait can be cast any distance without tearing off the hook. Thawing is rapid in saltwater, so a perfectly good, perhaps slightly out-of-season bait, can be presented at long casting range where it can catch a fish that you may need desperately!

Highwater mark

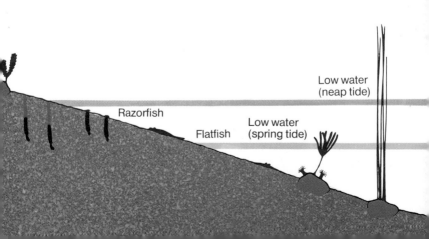

Razorfish

Flatfish

Low water (spring tide)

Low water (neap tide)

There will be a number of small fish lurking among the rocks and weed at the low tide mark. All of them will make hookbaits. The gobies, blennies and butterfish are found on any rocky shore, especially where the receding tide leaves rock pools containing weed and minute food animals to support them. The tiny fish make good float-fished baits for bass, rock codling and pollack. The rock pools are also a haven for shrimps. Small and transparent, they are rarely large enough to be used as a hookbait. It is to the sandy shore that we have to travel to get the size of shrimp bait needed.

Left *The largest lugworm are usually found down in the mud and sand near the low-tide mark. On gently sloping beaches or mudflats this can sometimes be a very long walk.* Right *These mud whorls are an indication of the presence of lugworm.*

Bait on the sandy shore

This environment produces a wealth of food when covered by the tide. Thousands of animals live in the sand and only emerge with a freshening tidal flow. Others, like the cockle and lugworm, lie beneath the sand surface, feeding on plankton that is drawn down into a burrow to be filtered through the body. Some creatures project part of their body above the sand in order to feed. On the sandy shore the angler must rake or dig for his bait.

Worms on the shore

Unless highly polluted, most stretches of sandy shore will have a resident population of lugworm. Their presence is indicated by a mass of tiny heaps of sand, looking like whirls of thick thread, interspersed by round depressions with a hole in the middle. The lugworm lies in a U-shaped tunnel, its head nearest to the hole. When the beach is covered with water, the worm comes close to the surface but sinks down to the bottom of the burrow at ebb tide. The largest worms are generally found nearest to the waterline.

There are two ways to dig for lug. When there are worm casts in profusion, trench digging pays off. Start by digging a single row for a length of about 6 ft (2 m). Use a stout garden fork, not a spade. The fork will lift solid sand without breaking any worms that are disturbed. A spade will cut lugworm, releasing the body contents. Never put damaged lug into the bait can, they will kill the healthy ones.

As the trench is dug, watch for signs of the tunnels, seen as tubes with discoloration around the edges. The worms can be any distance down but around 12 in (30 cm) is average. Having completed the first line of holes, dig the second fairly quickly because any worms scared by the vibrations made by your digging will retreat back and down into the sand. Probably the best way to dig worms, without missing any, is to have at least three people doing the job and taking turns with the fork helps as this is a back-breaking task. One does the digging, with two spotters to locate the worms among the sand thrown up. It is surprising how many lug are missed when one is digging alone.

When you have collected sufficient bait for the day's fishing, always fill the holes after you. As well as the tidiness of the beach, the safety of other users must be considered. An accident to people wading out into shallow water and falling in holes dug by bait diggers can be the cause of them losing the right to dig in that area.

Lugworm can be dug for by concentrating on the individual casts. Dig one forkful at the side of the worm's blowhole, then the next at the side of the thrown-up cast. Easing up the sand will inevitably reveal some of the tunnel. The third forkful should have the worm contained in the lifted sand. If it isn't there, inspect the edges of the hole for evidence of its burrow. The worm has probably gone deeper down after detecting you. You'll just have to follow it down with the fork.

Baiting up

There are many kinds of lugworm, not separate species but each type of sandy beach seems to produce a worm with a different body texture. This can range from the hard black lug of large size to small red, watery worms. We need all kinds as bait, though some are harder to keep on the hook than others. The lugworm can be mounted as single or multiple

HOOKING A SINGLE LUG

MULTIPLE STRING OF LUG

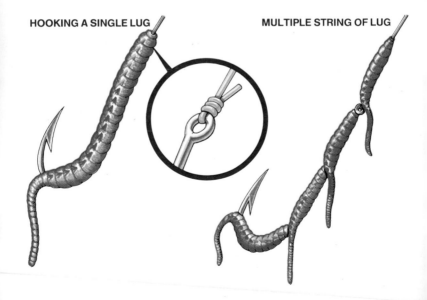

baits depending on what you are fishing for. Large lug suit a fairly long-shank hook tied on with a whisker of nylon left at the hook eye. When the worm is threaded onto the hook, the head is taken up over the hook eye and beyond the piece of nylon. Because it sticks out at right angles from the knot, the whisker helps to keep the worm in place. It also hides the hook shank completely, and a feeding fish will have to take the whole bait. Worms nicked onto the hook bend will be torn off very quickly by foraging sea fish.

Big fish prefer big baits. The cod should be given a huge mouthful. Half a dozen lugworm on a hook means that a lot of smell will be released into the water. If hung as a mass of worms from a hookbend, lug have a smell/taste value but are pulled off far too easily. I prefer to thread the worms over the hook and up the trace until I've built up what appears to be a lengthy worm. To get it, a cod has to take the hook and at least part of the line into its mouth. This means I'm fairly certain of hooking the fish effectively. Casting a big bait from the shore does cut down on the distance one can achieve but the amount of bait improves the chance of drawing a searching fish toward the offering.

Keeping lugworm
Lugworm dug for immediate use can safely be stored in a plastic bucket.

*Left **When hooking a single lugworm, leave a whisker of nylon when trimming the knot. This keeps the bait high on the hook. With a multiple lugbait, these are best threaded on the hook as a string rather than as a loose bunch.** Below **Keep lug separated when wrapping them in newspaper for storing.***

Clean the worms, throwing away all the injured ones. When fishing a hot, sunny day, add a small amount of seaweed to retain moisture. If the worms have to be retained for more than a day, they are best kept separate in dry newspaper. Lay them out in a line on the paper. Fold it into a pack without crushing the contents. Worms wrapped in this way can be kept for a few days in a fridge but never put them into the freezer compartment.

Raking the sand

Whenever I am plaice fishing, I feel that at least part of the bait must be cockles. Like lugworm, cockles live in sand lying just under the surface. They're easy to gather with a garden rake just as the tide falls away. At that time the cockle has extended its syphon to filter fine food particles from the shallow water. Cockles can be used on small hooks for flatfish or as an addition to lugworm, and give the added attraction of colour to a paternostered or legered bait. The bright orange part is the bit that attracts fish. Gather only as many as you need for bait, for it is difficult to keep cockles for more than a day or so. They can only be kept in perfect condition when immersed in a bucket of saltwater and *that* has to be constantly replenished. Keeping this and similar baits live and fresh is almost impossible for anglers living inland.

Razorfish

Razorfish are the last of the major baits to be gathered on the sandy shore. As their name suggests, they are distinctively shaped shellfish of the lower shore. They can only be collected at low water spring tides when the sea recedes far enough to uncover the beds. This is one bait that cannot be gathered from any sandy shore. It is localised, and you will have to learn of the few places in which it has established itself. Unfortunately, very little time is available at low water on a spring tide to get at the razorfish, so it is a matter of working fast.

Look for keyhole-shaped depressions in the wet sand. The razorfish lies deep down at the bottom of a perpendicular burrow. It can be spotted by the animal's habit of shooting a jet of water out of the hole when it feels unnatural vibrations, such as human footsteps. There are a number of ways in which the shellfish can be extracted from the burrow but I use the spear technique. It involves making a 3 ft (1 in) long spear of metal, the end hammered into an arrowhead with sharpened barbs. The razorfish lies in the hole upright, with the shells open, exposing the soft flesh. Push the spear down until you feel a resistance. A further sharp push will take the head of the spear clean through the open shells. The razorfish closes its shells around the shaft. All you have to do is give the spear a half turn so that the barbs are at right angles to the shells.

Spear

USING A RAZORFISH SPEAR

Left *Cockles are found in huge, localised beds. This shellfish makes an attractive hookbait for flatfish such as the flounder when estuary fishing. Thread a single large cockle onto a long-shank No. 2 hook.* Right *It looks crude—but it works. This very medieval-looking weapon with a barbed spear-head is the most successful method yet devised for extracting the razorfish from its burrow. The spear is pushed down the razorfish's burrow until it touches and passes through the creature's long twin shells. When the shaft is twisted, the barbs grip the two shells and then the razorfish can be pulled out.*

then draw it up to the surface. It seems an unlikely method, but it is an efficient way to collect this useful bait. Use razorfish by cutting the flesh into hook-size pieces. When boat fishing, a whole razorfish can be accommodated on a 6/0 hook.

Bait from a sand-mud mixture

Each of the former baits, either dug, raked or speared from a sandy shore will also be found in a sand-mud beach. The sandy shore is their perfect habitat but, as is usual in nature, some crossover between environments is usual. The sand-mud shore adds more bait species to our list. Ragworm of several species become an important bait. Digging them is much harder than collecting lug from the sandy beach. Rag inhabit the black, glutinous mire found at the bottom of harbours and in shallow estuaries. Small, red in colour, rag are a great hookbait for flatfish, bass and wrasse. Look for tiny holes in the mud. There will be no casts from ragworm as they feed in an entirely different way to the lugworm. Each worm makes a twisting maze of passages as it roams through the mud pursuing its carnivorous life style. The small red ragworm is brittle, so handle it with care. Use fine wire hooks for presentation, with the worm carefully threaded onto the shank. Ragworm works well when used as

BAIT-GATHERING ZONE ON A MUD/SAND SHORE
A prolific bait habitat

Mussels

Ragworm

Shrimps

Above *The king ragworm needs careful handling. The largest ones make a number of single baits. It can reach 15 in (40 cm) long and its pincers will inflict a painful wound.* Below *The sand-mud habitat is the home of many bait-worthy creatures.*

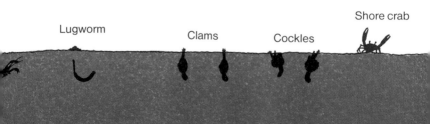

Lugworm Clams Cockles Shore crab

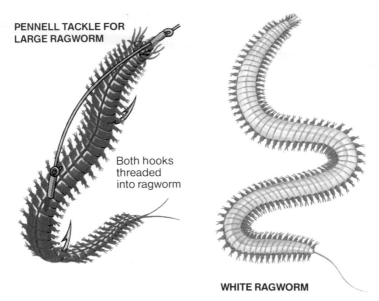

PENNELL TACKLE FOR LARGE RAGWORM

Both hooks threaded into ragworm

WHITE RAGWORM

pieces, but remember to get the whole of the worm section onto the hook and leave no free stump for fish to pull on.

King rag is a name given by anglers to the massive ragworm found among stones, under boulders and within thick clumps of exposed seaweed. It is found much closer to the water's edge than the smaller ragworms. This worm can grow to 18 in (45 cm) or so. Beware of the sharp pincers at the head. They can pack quite a nip. A worm of this size is a bit too big to be cast from the shore but it will break up into many smaller baits. Like the small ragworm the king rag loses little value as a bait when cut into sections, and there are times when it is best to use the whole worm. It can either be threaded over the hook and up the trace or a tandem hook rig can be used. The hooks get a better purchase on the worm if each one is threaded into the worm rather than being pushed through it. Another advantage in the two-hook rig is that shy fish may pluck at a large worm and tear the tail off. The Pennell tackle offers a second hook low down at the tail of the worm, which improves the hooking possibilities.

Sea match anglers cry their praises of the white ragworm. But it isn't a ragworm at all, just a member of a different group of bristleworms called catworms. Without doubt the white rag can be a competition winner

Far left *With two hooks, the Pennell tackle, named after H.C. Pennell, a 19th Century author and designer of a number of tackle set-ups still used today, gives a good hookhold when large ragworm is to be the bait. The two hooks hold the worm firmly and prevent it squirming up into a ball on a single hook. Pennell tackle was originally devised for pike and perch fishing in freshwater but it adapted very well for sea angling purposes.* Left *Anglers call this bait the white ragworm, but it is in fact a catworm. What matters is its value as a bait.* Right *The gaper works its way deep down into the mud and sand, but can be collected easily.*

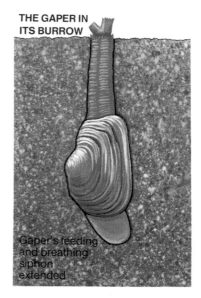

THE GAPER IN ITS BURROW

Gaper's feeding and breathing siphon extended

that attracts a wide variety of fish. It is quite commonly found near to and within lugworm beds, and digging for it is similar to the techniques when trenching for lugworm. This is another worm that does not indicate its presence with a cast. You'll have to dig and turn a lot of sand over. One disadvantage of this delicate little worm is that it has to remain in water if it is to stay alive. Some form of container that doesn't leak is needed if the worms are to be taken any distance in a car.

The other species of ragworm will live for long periods in a wooden box or plastic container packed with a couple of layers of wet seaweed. Some anglers wrap them in newspaper but it isn't a good idea because the worms suffer from a lack of air.

Another beautiful bait that can be dug from a sand-mud shore is the gaper, or clam. You can recognize clam territory by the large blowhole made by the creature to extrude its syphon when feeding. The gaper lies buried at about 9 in (23 cm) deep. It's a big bait, fleshy yet quite tough when the shells are prised apart. I like it when shore fishing as it stays on the hook, even in the roughest wave pattern. This is a perfect bait for bass, and small pieces will lure flounders and other flatfish. Clams can be kept out of water for about a day as the seal around the shell edges prevents them drying out too quickly.

SANDEEL ON A FLOWING TRACE

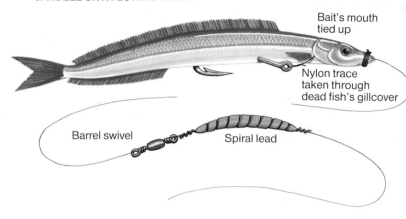

Bait's mouth tied up

Nylon trace taken through dead fish's gillcover

Barrel swivel

Spiral lead

As the mud turns to a coarser, more sandy material near to the water's edge, we can expect to find sandeels. At low water, small specimens can be raked out of the sand but is in the permanent shallows that the bigger specimens will be found. They can be caught with a metal scythe-shaped tool, called a vingler in the West Country, that is swept round in wide strokes just under the sand. When a resistance is felt to the sweep of the tool, the fingers of the other hand are run along the blade until the fish is found. A positive finger pressure holds the sandeel trapped. Larger sandeel are found farther offshore, where they are netted or taken on strings of tiny feathers.

The sandeel can be used in a variety of ways: under a float from a rock fishing mark, as a legered bait for rays, small tope, turbot and other fish-eating predators, or as a livebait over a pinnacle reef. Mounted on a nylon trace a sandeel can be trolled or worked sink-and-draw over ground known to hold pollack. As a constantly worked bait, I like to use a freshly killed sandeel mounted on a long flowing trace with the addition of a spiral weight, just heavy enough to get the bait down to work in the tide. Take the hook through the mouth and out of the gillcase and nick it through the belly of the bait in front of the anal fin. When trolled or fished sink-and-draw, the bait's mouth should be wired up with soft copper wire to prevent water pushing through the gills for the constant water pressure would soon rip the bait from the trace. Hooked in this way, the sandeel will spin slowly, needing a single barrel swivel to take out any line twist.

To simulate a live sandeel swimming we need to troll erratically, because sandeels swim erratically. Try to vary the speed of the troll by steering a zigzag course. Each 90-degree turn will slow the bait, letting it almost stop in the water before pulling ahead.

Over a reef, the sandeel comes into its own as a *worked* bait. Mount it in exactly the same fashion with a trace of only 4 ft (1 m) beyond the swivel. Drop the bait down until the reef is felt or until an echo sounder gives the accurate depth reading. Take in a couple of winds to stop the bait becoming entangled in any weed fronds rising up from the reef. The rod action should be a slow raising of the rod tip through an arc of about 6–8 ft (1.8–2.4 m). Stop the movement of the rod, hold it still, then lower it quickly back to where the rod arc began. At the same time, take in a couple of winds of line. If the reef is in shallow water continue the action all the way up. In deeper water, the bait can be lowered to begin the sink-and-draw when you think that the bait is too far above the reef to be followed. In late evening, I continue the bait retrieval to the surface,

Left *The sandeel needs just enough weight to enable it to be cast from boat or shore and also to get it down well below the surface.*
Below *Successful trolling depends upon a vertical zig-zag pattern made by the lure rising and falling through the water.*

ZIG-ZAG TROLLING METHOD

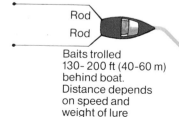

Rod
Rod
Baits trolled
130- 200 ft (40-60 m)
behind boat.
Distance depends
on speed and
weight of lure

because pollack rise in the water as the sun goes down. Their vertical migration matches that of the small fry that swim up to the surface to feed on plankton.

Sandeels can be frozen down for use in winter. Although all frozen fish go mushy after thawing out, these small fish seem to stay firm for longer than those other favourites, herring and mackerel.

Prawns and shrimps

Both of these free-swimming crustaceans can be taken from a wide variety of habitats. Among the rocks there will always be pools, refreshed with every tide, from which prawns and shrimps can be caught. In the shallows, with water up to your knees, prawns and shrimps can be gathered out of the sand with a fine-meshed net. They lie with only the feelers waving above the sand.

Both prawns and shrimps are fished best as livebaits. They do take fish when dead but it is the action—a wild, erratic motion—that gives the live prawn or shrimp its attractiveness. Obviously, it is a bait that must be seen by feeding fish. For that reason, I use both baits on float-fished

Shrimps and prawns should always be hooked through the tail section. This way, they are able to move attractively in the water.

HOOKING PRAWN AND SHRIMP

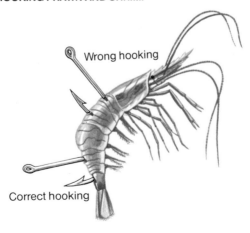

Wrong hooking

Correct hooking

Mackerel, when fresh, are probably the best sea angling bait.

rigs. The bait is nicked through the tail, just ahead of where it fans out, leaving the arched body clear of the hook. I find that fish do not grab at these baits. Whether the movement of legs and feelers make the fish wary I don't know. What you get is an initial inspection of the hookbait, often seen as a bouncing float for a few seconds, before fish take the shrimp. Probably the exaggerated movement of the bait, suspended off the bottom by the float, is new behaviour to fish. The usual reaction of any shrimp or prawn is to scurry off to cover.

Baits found offshore

Of all the sea angler's baits, mackerel must be the most successful. Full of oil, with minute scales that flash in the light as they drift downtide, the mackerel is a bait that we have to fish for. The shoals are distributed around the entire British Isles during the months of June to November. As winter comes, our mackerel gather in deep water in the seas off south-west Devon and Cornwall. Even there, the species knows no peace from predation by man. The commercial fishermen of many nations reap vast hauls to be sold on the European markets or converted into fish meal.

Feathering for bait

Mackerel are taken by jigging a string of feathered lures down through the depths. Where mackerel are depends on the availability of food. It

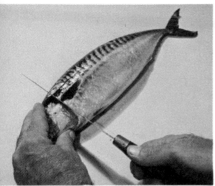

Above left *Hold the mackerel by the head and cut away from the hand towards the tail. This avoids nasty cuts if the blade slips off the backbone when the boat rolls.* Above *The knife must run along the ridged backbone to avoid wastage of the flesh.* Left *This produces a whole mackerel side.* Right *Mackerel feathers can be bought commercially from tackle shops, but they are easily made at home. The materials you need are chicken feathers, left white or dyed, hooks and nylon.*

takes a lot of natural food to provide enough to hold a travelling shoal of fish. Mackerel are plankton feeders but that doesn't mean that they only eat microscopic animals. The word plankton means life, animal and vegetable, that drifts on the ocean currents. Within that soup of rich protein are countless millions of small fish, so we anglers have provided ourselves with a multi-hook rig that represents a small shoal of fry.

Although called feathers, the string of lures can be constructed from a number of materials. Fine slivers of plastic tubing, strips of silver and gold foil, animal hair or unravelled string are all useful to dress the tinned hooks with. Bind the dressing onto the hooks with the whipping knot associated with spade-end hooks. I prefer using spade-ends as they

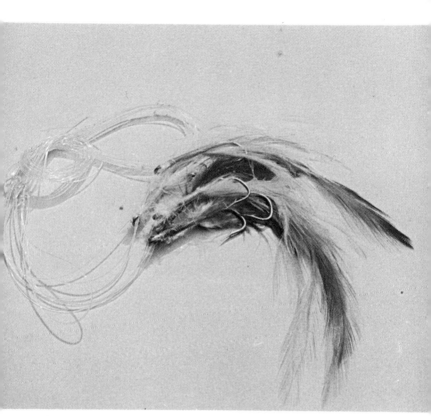

stand off straight from the nylon. Ringed hooks swivel at the point where the knot is tied. Six feathers is enough on any string. More than that and the rig becomes dangerous when hooked mackerel are thrashing around as they are brought in. Tie each feathered hook onto about 1 ft (15 cm) of 30-lb (13.5-kg) line. The main line should be of 45-lb (20-kg) nylon. This gives a stiff rig that doesn't tangle too easily. Feathers are subject to harsh treatment, so we need them to last for a few outings.

Take only as many mackerel from the sea as you really need. There is little point in filling a boat with these fish because it isn't angling, it's bait-gathering requiring little skill. The sea is not all bountiful, as we are beginning to find out, so let us conserve what we have.

Above *Three different methods of mackerel feather construction. Top, conventional feathers; centre, plastic tube bodies; bottom, the miniature sandeel.* Below *Take extra care when cutting bait at sea in a rolling boat. Always cut away from the hand steadying the bait.*

Preparing mackerel baits

The mackerel is a fish that can be used whole, as lashes, or cut into strips. Only the freshly caught fish will cut into perfect baits. Old mackerel, frozen fish or salted ones lose a great deal in attraction. Start by buying the best-quality bait knife that you can afford. Something that will take a perfect edge. The kind that rust slightly, made from Swedish steel, are often best. I certainly cannot get a stainless steel knife to match them for sharpness. One with a handle that floats is a good idea—you wouldn't believe the number of knives that go over the side of sea angling boats!

Lay the mackerel on a cutting board that will not slide around. Make the first cut behind the fish's gillcase, taking the blade down to the backbone. Hold the head of the bait and run the blade along the spine to the bait's tail. If you have to saw at the flesh, the knife is blunt! Always cut away from the hand that is holding the fish steady. Never risk cutting yourself badly when you are out fishing—it is a long way back to harbour and hospital!

The mackerel will give you two large lashes, one each side. Keep the head and skeleton as the former makes a good bait for conger and other scavengers while the white belly strip, left after filleting off the lashes, is a superb, tough hookbait. Fish a lash by taking the hook through the flesh twice. There is a difference of opinion about which end should be attached first. I prefer the fat end to be nearest the hook bend. Fresh mackerel lashes are firm and stay on the hook under strong current pressure but there are many species of fish, like tope, dogfish and conger that can rip a bait off without getting hooked. Their bait-stealing activities can be thwarted by tying the bait onto the trace with elasticated thread or soft copper wire.

When mounting a mackerel lash, make it doubly secure on the hook by tying it to the eye or trace with elasticated thread.

Smaller strip baits are cut from the lashes diagonally so that each bait has the darker green colour and a flash of the bait's white belly. This simulates, in miniature, the mackerel coloration. Always match the hook to the size of bait to ensure efficient hooking. Failure to do this is the largest single cause of loss of fish. The lash demands at least a 6/0 hook, with smaller strips fished on 4/0 and smaller hooks. Mackerel has a tough skin, which stays on the hook even though a feeding fish may well have stripped the flesh away. This happens mostly when the strip has been pulled down off the shank, onto the hook bend. Hooks that have the sliced shanks are an advantage when mounting fishbait because they hold the bait much higher up the hook shank, thus preventing the sucked-out strip.

Whole mackerel are used for the larger predatory species such as conger, shark and tope. Mount these baits using a baiting needle to lead the trace through from the mouth and out from the tail wrist of the mackerel. Doing this masks the trace material, which could be cable-laid wire, and buries the bulk of hook shank and bend within the bait. Perfect presentation is vital on those seemingly many occasions when fish are shy in biting. Apart from the conger, most predators inspect baits carefully before taking them. Tope pick a bait up, mouth it and drop it quickly if they suspect it. Shark will often worry a float-fished bait for ten minutes or so before a positive take occurs. The other advantage in this baiting system is that the bait isn't easily torn away from the terminal rig either by casting or by strong, determined fish. Additional security can be gained by tying the bait to the trace wire with an inch or two of elasticated thread or even wool.

Far left *Cut mackerel diagonally into strips so that each one has a dark blue and silver part. This produces a life-like flash in the water.* Left *Ten fine strips can be cut from a side of mackerel— but the bait-knife must be very sharp and therefore needs to be handled carefully.* Right *With careful preparation and intelligent use of the knife, mackerel make a really first-class bait for all species of sea fish.*

A whole mackerel, especially when gleaming fresh from the sea, is the ideal shark bait. At death, this irridescence quickly dies away.

WHOLE MACKEREL RIG FOR SHARK AND TOPE FISHING

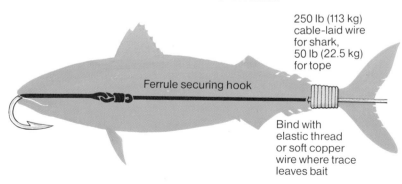

250 lb (113 kg) cable-laid wire for shark, 50 lb (22.5 kg) for tope

Ferrule securing hook

Bind with elastic thread or soft copper wire where trace leaves bait

Herring baits

This is the second best sea angling fishbait but one that has to be caught for us by the trawler or drift netter. Herrings can be caught on feathers though I cannot guarantee you will catch many! Even when frozen, herrings are never as good as freshly caught mackerel. The flesh is softer but contains almost as much oil. As whole fish baits, I like to mount the herring in a similar way to deadbaiting in freshwater, using two treble *sea-sized* hooks. The trace is again baited through the flesh at the tail and tied off with thread. The method is suitable for constant sink-and-draw fishing over reefs for ling, big cod and pollack, all fish that can be lured away from the reef by a fluttering bait.

Cutting herring into lashes and strips isn't easy when the fish is soft. Try cutting up this bait *before* freezing it down. The strips are laid out on greaseproof paper then rolled up ready for storage. Putting a hook in is slightly easier when the bait is still a little frozen. Salting herring bait down improves the toughness of the skin a little, but this soon fades when the bait has been in the water for a short time. Baits for shorecasting can be held on the hook by stopping the threaded-on

The sea angling counterpart of the minnow sink-and-draw bait, here a herring, but other species can also be used with effect.

HERRING BAIT SINK-AND-DRAW RIG

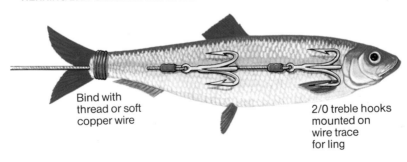

Bind with thread or soft copper wire

2/0 treble hooks mounted on wire trace for ling

herring strip with a really tough shellfish, such as the whelk, which sits solidly on the hookbend and prevents the strip from sliding down.

Sprats

The sprat makes a good casting and legered bait when used whole. The secret is to mount it onto the hook with a loop of nylon trapping the tail against the hook shank. Sprats are another soft-bodied baitfish and without a tying-on system they almost fall off a hook. But fish, such as winter cod, take them avidly, so a little care in presentation will pay off. When fishing for smaller species such as whiting, which take sprat bait well, cut the fish diagonally into little chunks across the body. The bait gives more security if hooked through the firmer flesh surrounding the backbone.

Fishbait as attractors

Mackerel, herring and sprats have two things in common; they are shoal fish and immensely oily. The predators are conditioned to follow the shoals and hunt them by sight and smell. We can adopt groundbaiting tactics to match this feeding behaviour. Called rubby dubby, mashed fish of any of these species is used as an attractor.

Sprats are a soft-bodied baitfish and need careful attachment to the terminal rig if they are to stay on the hook during the cast.

HOOKING A WHOLE SPRAT OR A SMALL HERRING

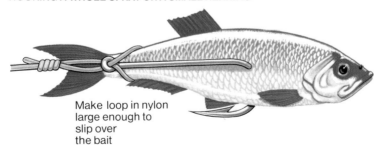

Make loop in nylon
large enough to
slip over
the bait

The anchored method

Cod, ray or tope fishing can be made more effective by streaming rubby dubby down the tide for fish to detect. As all three species, and incidentally many others, feed on or close to the seabed, we put our rubby dubby into a bait tin attached to the anchor chain. A receptacle such as a large, empty paint tin, with holes punched around the sides, is ideal. Add a little sawdust to the mess of of pounded fish flesh and offal to act as a carrier for the oil. It will absorb a lot of it, keeping it down on the bottom rather than letting the oily droplets float up to mid-water.

Shark anglers, especially those who go out to drift for blue shark, use a surface rubby dubby technique. An onion net, or one with a suitably wide mesh, is filled with near-liquid fish remains. It's tied onto the boat's hull so that all the slight movements dip the sack below the waves to release a constant stream of oily pieces. The bulk of the oil floats on the surface while the pounded flesh particles sink slowly through the

RUBBY-DUBBY FROM AN ANCHORED BOAT

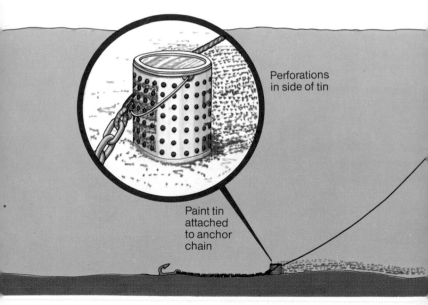

Perforations in side of tin

Paint tin attached to anchor chain

water. Sharks follow this rubby trail whether they are near the surface or deeper down among mackerel shoals. Bran or sawdust will help to carry the oil deeper in the water, at the same time providing a rain of minute feed particles that the fish will investigate. There are times when shark swim deep and porbeagle particularly are a species that favour greater depth, especially when in the vicinity of an underwater reef. Here, our rubby dubby needs some sand to give it a faster rate of sink. Ideally, the hookbait ought to be suspended within the mainstream of the rubby dubby. But it isn't always necessary as shark, when they detect the rubby dubby trail, circle around to find where the stuff is coming from.

Blood and animal offal from an abbatoir can be added to rubby dubby and is a valuable addition to the groundbaiting effect. Shark are credited with being able to smell blood over immense distances, even at dilutions of just a few parts per million of water. So when sharking, anything that looks or smells like their food is worth collecting for the fishing trip!

Shark fishing while at anchor, using legered rubby dubby as an attractor. Shark can detect it from very long distances.

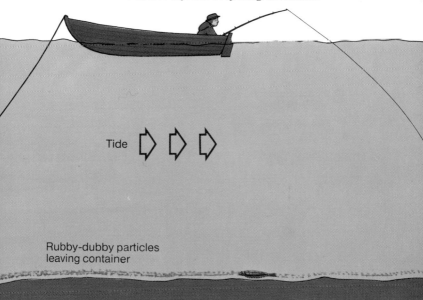

Tide

Rubby-dubby particles leaving container

RUBBY-DUBBY SACHETS ATTACHED TO RIG AND PUNCTURED BY NAIL

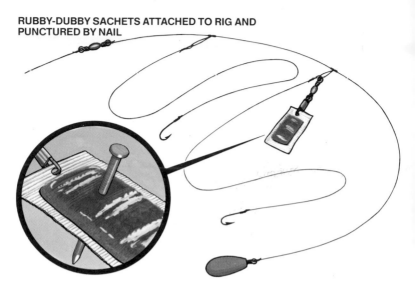

Rubby dubby sachets can be attached to a paternoster rig.

RUBBY-DUBBY ON THE DRIFT

Oil slick on surfac

Suspended
mackerel
bait

Improving the hookbait

Fishing from a charter boat doesn't always allow the use of rubby dubby. When sharking, the skipper controls the methods of groundbaiting and few skippers would want the additional labour of lowering a rubby tin on the anchor warp. But the angler can do something for himself. Small sachets of mashed fish and oil can be tied to the hook as droppers on the terminal rig.

Even small polythene bags filled with rubby will improve the angler's chances. They are simple to set up and prepare for use. Just before lowering it to the seabed, pierce the bag with a nail so that the current washes the contents out in a progressive stream.

Old worms that have dried out can be improved by injecting them with pilchard oil. Any bait can be improved by adding fish-oil as it is probably the most powerful attractor that we have. I've frequently caught more fish than my companions by soaking shellfish, limpets particularly, in a dish of pilchard oil for a few minutes. Of course, the oil soon washes out but while it is present it encourages otherwise lethargic fish to leave their resting places in search of a meal.

Using rubby dubby to create a scent-lane while drifting for shark.

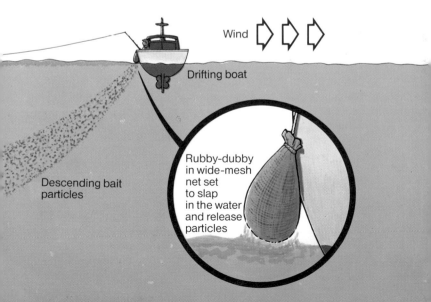

Wind

Drifting boat

Descending bait particles

Rubby-dubby in wide-mesh net set to slap in the water and release particles

Squid and cuttlefish

In tropical waters, anglers set out to catch both these baits by using a miniature replica of the squid. This is a jig with a number of lethal prongs mounted below a lead body, and they take live squids by the hundred. In European waters we rely on the commercial fishing industry to send their squid catches to market. Unfortunately for anglers, the squid has begun to figure on restaurant menus and the dining tables of our immigrant population. This has raised the price of what used to be a cheap bait. So the small squids, just right for cod fishing, are now imported from California! But the squid, and to a lesser extent the cuttlefish, make useful alternative baits to worms and fish. They are specially effective when fish have become satiated on a bait that occurs seasonally, such as the times when cod are jammed full of sprats. Offer the cod a sprat hookbait then and you are wasting your time, but a strip of squid often gets grabbed eagerly.

There is no waste when using squid, they cut up into a variety of different-sized baits that can be repeatedly frozen. Unlike fish that doesn't stay usable for more than a few months, and certainly cannot be re-frozen if not used up on a fishing trip, squid can be carried home to freeze again. It seems to have an indeterminate freezer life.

Prepare squid strip by carefully slitting open the conical mantle. Scrap out the organs before slicing the body flesh into strips. The ten arms, covered with suckers, can be fished as a bunch although I have never found them to be as effective as the mantle flesh. Squid is tough, so it stays on the hook but I'm not sure that it has anything other than a sight-feeding attraction to fish. This bait becomes more useful if you add a tippet of lugworm or a strip of fish. Lying on the bottom, a squid bait will be taken by cod and rays but I have found that it succeeds more as a driftlined strip bait, or offered on a flowing trace to fish that swim and feed in mid-water.

The sea angler's bait farm

Farming sea bait is not really practical. Most live baits have to be fed if they are to stay in perfect condition and that is something that we cannot easily do. But it is possible to simulate a saltwater habitat capable of supporting bait for a short period without feeding the inhabitants. Ragworm can be kept in an aquarium. The saltwater can be kept fresh by topping up, if you live near to the coast, or manufactured from artificial material sold in sacks to aquaria and laboratory users. It is vital to provide sufficient oxygenation. The small pumps sold at tropical fish shops can do this. Kept this way, ragworm will remain in fair condition for at least a couple of weeks. There is a natural body wastage because

SQUID AND CUTTLEFISH

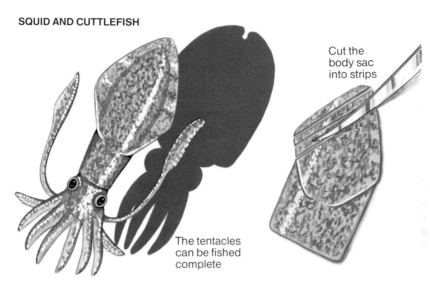

Cut the body sac into strips

The tentacles can be fished complete

Squid and cuttlefish are often used in conjunction with lugworm. But scrape the mottled surface skin off the body of the squid before putting it on the hook.

they cannot be supplied with the food of a carnivorous invertebrate.

At the soft-back stage crabs can also be kept for a week or so. They do not need saltwater but the habitat has to remain damp. A plentiful supply of seaweed will provide the essential conditions needed for the crabs to remain healthy. While growing the new shell they do not eat to the same extent as the hard crab, but there must still be a deterioration in the quality of the creature.

In my opinion, the sea angler would be better to look to methods of farming a bait crop. Crabs can be encouraged to use man-made hiding places. Pieces of earthenware pipe make perfect holes for crabs if set into mud among weed and small rocks. Choice of where the farming takes place is the difficulty, if one is to create a source of bait *and* ensure that it isn't gathered by somebody else!

Artificial lures

If we discount the game fisherman's flies, it would be true to say that more fish are consistently taken on artificial baits by sea anglers than by any other fishermen. One could successfully fish an entire season without recourse to natural baits. Basically, the reason for this is that there are many more species in saltwater that feed by killing fish smaller than themselves. The key to success is the action given to a lure, coupled with a knowledge of the environment. Some artificial lures are made to accurately resemble something in nature, but bits of metal, a bunch of feathers or a length of plastic tubing can be given that essential movement which makes them fish catchers!

Lures for the shore angler

Spinning is an important part of the shore angler's sport. His lures and methods differ little from those used by a coarse or game fisherman. Any differences in the metal baits will be of size and weight. By the sea, casting a lure can be more difficult because of the increased wind speeds associated with the coastline. When difficulty is experienced, changing to a larger lure to get greater casting weight only compounds the problem. Ideally, a heavier but same-size lure is necessary. Some

The most successful sea angling lures are those that move with an undulating action. Both the Toby and Shanny lures produce such an action, a reflection of their popularity.

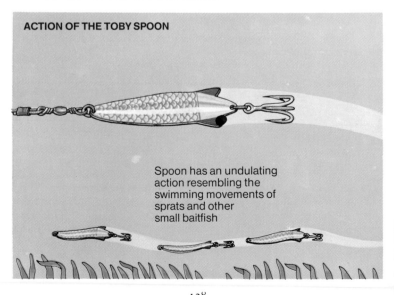

ACTION OF THE TOBY SPOON

Spoon has an undulating action resembling the swimming movements of sprats and other small baitfish

makers of spinning lures provide for this. The Toby spoon and the Shanny lure are two baits that have different thicknesses, giving varying weight lures for the same size and surface area.

The wobbling spoon is the most effective metal lure for spinning from the shore. Simulating the erratic motion of a wounded fish, it will take pollack, bass and cod, all species that come close-in within casting range. Oddly enough, the blade spinner doesn't seem to be effective in the sea. The wave motion affects the way in which they work, adding peculiar characteristics not seen in the same lure when used in freshwater.

There is one bar spoon that has stood the test of time among sea spinners: the German sprat has the unique properties of a perfect action, looking like the irregular swimming movement of the sandeel, and good casting because of its narrow shape but high weight. If anything, this bait can be said to fulfill all the shore angler's demands. And, it takes fish used either as a spinning lure or trailed behind a boat.

There can be very few sea anglers that would not think in terms of

The German sprat—a first-class sea spinning lure. Attach the hook as shown in the lower lure, the curved shape will give a realistic action as it is drawn through the water.

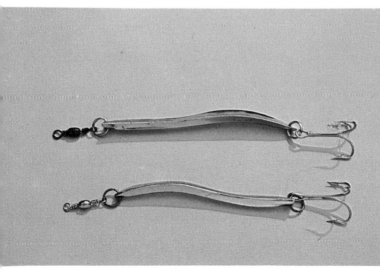

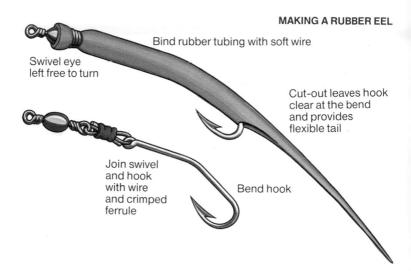

Bind rubber tubing with soft wire

Swivel eye
left free to turn

Cut-out leaves hook
clear at the bend
and provides
flexible tail

Join swivel
and hook
with wire
and crimped
ferrule

Bend hook

rubber eels as a spinning or sink-and-draw bait. We have come a long way from those early 'gaspipe' eels that were the standby of many bass fishers. In fact, more effort has been put in by tackle manufacturers to develop artificial eels than in all the other lure types. Since this is a book concerned with doing things for yourself, I will include the make-up for the simple rubber or plastic tube eel because I feel that it is worthy of continued consideration. If it has a fault, it lies in the motion forcing a fish to grab a bait that can be spinning quite fast. This doesn't lead to achieving a perfect hookhold.

Most artificial eels designed in the last decade do not spin. They wobble slightly, and have a fast thrashing tail. Made from new plastics, the lures are tough yet have very flexible tails that will flutter enticingly in the gentle flow of the slackest tide. Made originally for spinning and trolling, the lures achieved such success that they are now produced in huge sizes and numbers for taking specimen fish over wrecks and other prolific big fish marks. They score heavily over metal lures in that they do not have to be worked or trolled at speed to achieve optimum action—the manufacturer has built all the action into this artificial animal.

Artificial eels, such as the Redgill, Eddystone and Ailsa Craig, have no

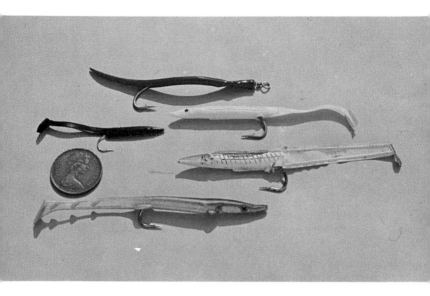

Above left *This simple home-made lure, the rubber eel, can be put together with ease.* Above *A group of artificial sandeels: (top to bottom) a rubber tubing eel, Delta eels, an Eddystone eel and the very popular Redgill.*

weight so they need the addition of a spiral or similar weight uptrace. With other metal lures, this would result in a severe dampening of action, but it doesn't happen with the eels. Sufficient attraction is built into the body to overcome the addition of the lead. Add the spinning weight at least 4 ft (1 m) ahead of the bait and make sure that is a dull colour. A new, flashing lead will often be attacked by the fish.

I've never had any real success using plugs while spinning in saltwater. There have been times when a trolled diving plug of the Rapala type has pulled a few pollack but generally the plug's action is upset by the complex currents that affect the shoreline. This, plus the inevitable weight needed to assist casting a weightless plug, kills the action stone dead. The Rapala, or its many copies, does have a use when trolling offshore in a dinghy. Its action suits trolling and the fish-like appearance goes a long way to giving the lure a high rating.

We've seen many plastic worms, fish and unspeakable objects come

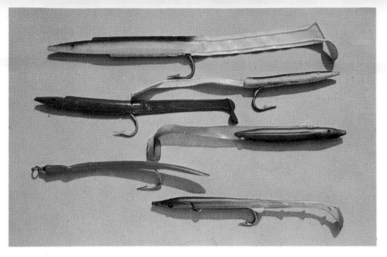

Above *Large artificial sandeels for wreckfishing (top to bottom); Eddystone, Ailsa Craig, Eddystone, Delta, plastic tube eel and the Redgill.* Below *Most artificial sandeels are supplied with a suitably sized hook, which must be attached to the wire trace.* Right *Variations on the Rapala, a lure that has been extensively copied but rarely surpassed as a highly efficient, taking lure.*

ARTIFICIAL SANDEEL AND TRACE

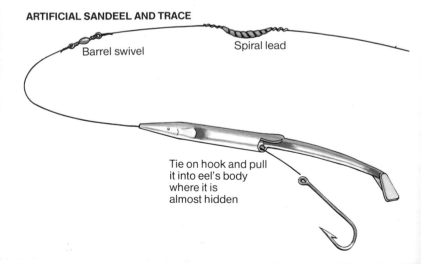

Barrel swivel

Spiral lead

Tie on hook and pull it into eel's body where it is almost hidden

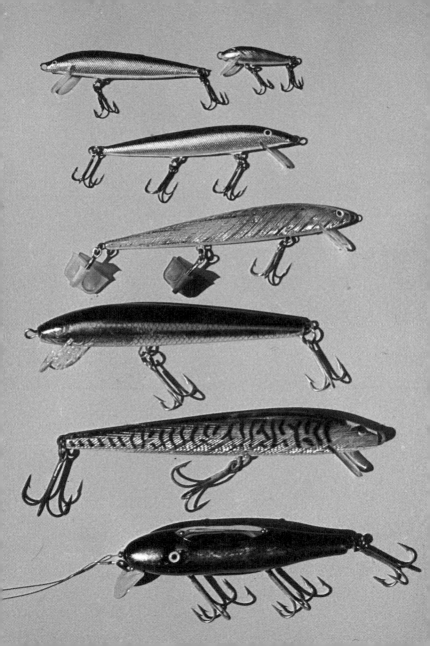

into tackle shops over the years. Almost all of them have proved useless with the exception of the Twister. I first saw them ten years ago in Japan, where they were being made for the American market. Inevitably, they arrived in Britain and have proved enormously successful as both a spinning and trolling lure for pollack in particular. Used threaded on a hook trace, with no lead, they spin so fast that they kink the line terribly. But fix them on a jighead that is balanced to swim a definite way up and the Twister becomes another animal! I troll them and cast them when fishing known pollack water.

I always treat trolling as a form of spinning. The lures are similar except when huge fish are expected. We are unfortunate when seeking big-game species in our waters. The North Atlantic waters do contain some tunny, the occasional broadbill swordfish and sharks, but nobody

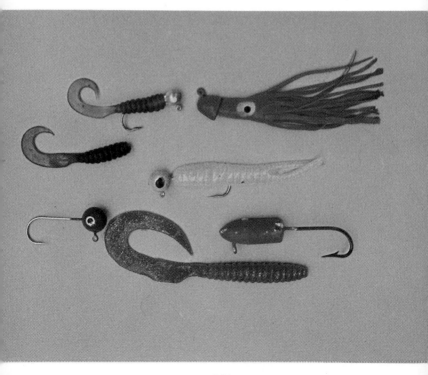

would seriously suggest that we troll for them. The porbeable shark is, to my knowledge, the only fish that has been consistently taken by trolling techniques using mackerel baits. Whether they will take a legitimate big-game lure is questionable. The sharks have to be feeding on the surface for lures to have a chance and, of course, the trolling boat cannot entice the fish up with the usual rubby tactics!

Below left The plastic popping lures originated from the demands of sportfishermen in America, a country not unknown for colourful innovation. They need a jighead for casting. Below Two big-game trolling lures for sailfish, marlin and tunny. These species are rarely if ever seen in UK waters, but smaller lures may well attract surface feeding shark in the south west.

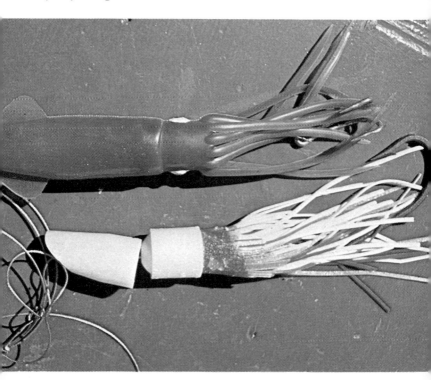

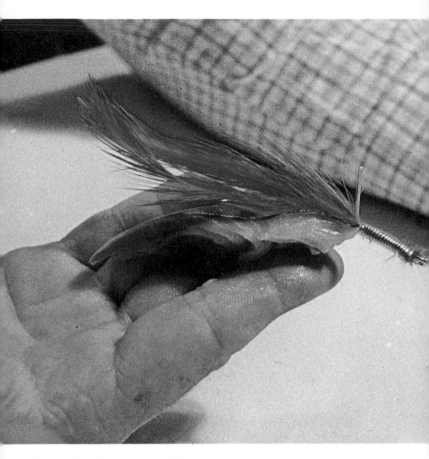

Lures for the deepsea fisher

At one time the only artificial lures we used when out boat fishing were feathers to catch bait. From this early lure pollack and cod feathers were developed, although they are only larger editions of the mackerel fly. Baiting the feathers became a ritual among cod anglers. The feather to simulate a small fish, with the bait providing smell and taste. A proven method is to fish three feathered lures, each with a small worm or strip of fresh fish bait as a tippet to the hook.

I've experimented with pollack and cod flies fished over the tops of wrecks and pinnacle reefs. They work well on a long flowing trace when dropped back over the underwater mass. To provide a real mouthful, the flies have to be heavily dressed. Like sandeel, only the tail has any real movement. Suitable hooks can be had from a tackle shop selling salmon low-water hooks. Add a Lurex body with a wing of stiff, bucktail fibres. A fly tied onto a 4/0 hook is about the right size. Again, additional weight is needed to get the lure down to where fish are, yet it has little effect on the action of the fly.

*Left **The traditional feathers can be transformed into a more attractive lure by the presence of slips of mackerel or shellfish on the hooks. This creates the baited feather—in effect, feathers with visual attraction** and **taste.** Below **These are the basic materials for tying your own pollack flies: thread, badger hair, lurex thread for the body, wool and dope.***

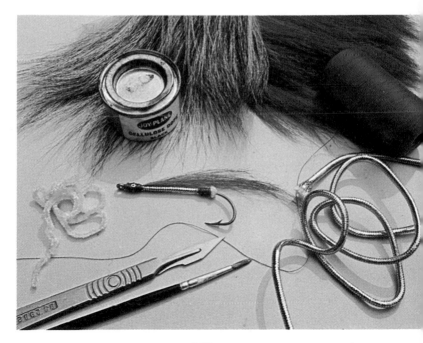

Fishing from a dinghy

The dinghy angler has a much better chance to try new tactics than his counterpart fishing from a charter boat. He can fly-fish for pollack and bass, troll to his heart's content and freeline natural or artificial baits in the slack waters of saltwater creeks and estuaries. It is from a dinghy that the art of the baited spoon is best carried out. The technique involves casting a spoon, mounted on a fixed flight and attached to a single hook. Ragworm or lug is used as the hookbait. The spoon is slowly wound in, causing it to flutter over a sand or mud seabed, sending up flurries of colour in the water. Flatfish feed by watching intently for signs of worms that have emerged from the bottom. Seeing the spurts of sand, they follow the baited spoon. The method works perfectly in shallow water. In a current, such as would be found fishing from an anchored boat in a river mouth, the baited spoon is lowered to flutter in the water flow just

off the bottom. The constant turning of the blade is seen by fish that are lying on the estuary bed or searching for food. No retrieval of the spoon is necessary, just keep the baited rig fluttering away above the bottom.

This lure spins for long periods and can put a lot of line twist into your gear. Put at least two good swivels into the rig to alleviate this problem. Many of the better baited spoon rigs have a train of swivels separating the spoon from the rig and baited hook. The system is highly recommended for flounders, but will attract many other shallow-water species.

Below left The flounder spoon is a highly effective fishing weapon *when coupled with a piece of ragworm on the hook. A little mackerel spinner (top) can be trolled or cast with the addition of a spinning weight.* Below *How to fish the flounder spoon.*

THE BAITED SPOON

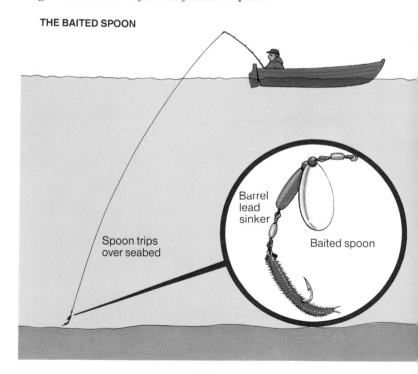

Spoon trips over seabed

Barrel lead sinker

Baited spoon

Wrecking

A selection of specialised artificial lures have been devised specifically for fishing over deepwater wrecks and reefs. The depths can be anything up to 50 fathoms, demanding a lot of weight to sink the bait efficiently. The first of the lures came from Norway, where they are used commercially to catch cod and ling. Called pirks, they are either moulded from lead or cast in steel. Weights range from 4 oz to 2 lb (113 g–1 kg) or more, which makes them expensive to use and to lose! Apart from providing the jigging motion there is little that the angler can do to impart an attractive movement. It is all up to the designer of the pirk.

The shapes vary somewhat as does the colour. What is vital is that a pirk should represent a fish's movements above the wreck. Colour is unnecessary as at the depths pirking is carried out in, there are no discernible colours. A flashing, silvery appearance is needed.

Angling on the bottom with fishbait can be improved by the addition of metal attractors. Tied into a paternostered rig small spoon blades will ensure that the arrival of your bait is more clearly seen. There is no need to give the flashers life by jigging the terminal rig up and down. Seabed currents will give the spoon blades enough movement to make them work. Insert a barrel swivel between the main trace and hook dropper to remove line twist created by the action of the blade.

Conclusion

There are thousands of baits and metal lures, all of which will take a fish at sometime or other. I have concerned myself with proven fish catchers that are readily available. It doesn't end there. My advice is to try anything on a hook, because the whole business of fishing is about experimenting. To catch a fish on a lure that you made or a natural food discounted by the experts adds immeasurably to the fun of fishing.

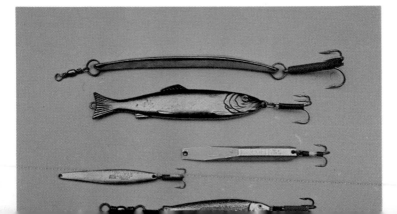

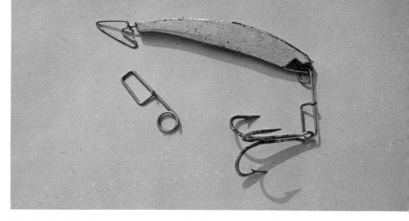

Above *Treble hooks can be attached to lures and rigs by Positive Poundage Links. When the link parts, only the hook is lost when it snags, rather than the body of the probably expensive pirk. Below left A selection of the wide range of pirks available. Below Flashers are a useful addition to paternostered rigs, because fish hunt by sight as well as detecting food by smell.*

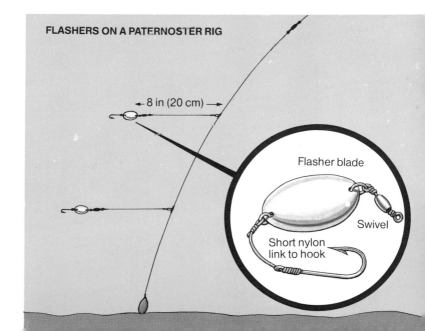

FLASHERS ON A PATERNOSTER RIG

← 8 in (20 cm) →

Flasher blade

Swivel

Short nylon link to hook

BAIT CHARTS

The Coarse Angler's Baits

Worms

Lobworms	Found in lawns and close-cropped meadows.
Redworms	Live in manure heaps.
Brandlings	Found in compost heaps.

Maggots and other grubs

Commercial maggots	Can be bought in a variety of colours.
Pinkies	Used as hook or feeder baits.
Squatts	Feeder maggots.
Gozzers	Home-produced special hookbaits.
Sour bran specials	Ideal bait for the DIY angler.
Casters	The chrysalis stage in the life cycle of all maggots.
Bloodworms	Larvae of the midge.
Jokers	Gnat larvae.
Wasp grubs	Not a bait to trifle with!
Docken grubs	Larvae of the ghost moth.
Caterpillars	Larval stage of butterflies and moths.
Caddis grubs	Larvae of sedge flies.
Mealworms	Grubs of flour beetle.

Insects

Beetles	Can be used as a dapping bait.
Moths	Useful as a dapping hookbait in the evening for chub.
Trout angler's flies	Sedge and mayflies are large enough to put onto a hook, other smaller Ephemerids are a little difficult.
Grasshoppers	A very active dapping lure.
Earwigs	Can be gathered by filling an upturned flowerpot with straw and placing it on a stick, especially among dahlias.

High protein additives for both groundbait and hookbait

Blood	Used, in the past, by tench fishers.
Catfood	Added for its meat and taste value.
Dogfood	Added for its meat and taste value.
PYM	Phillips Yeast Mixture.
Beemax	Wheat germ.
Casilan	Calcium caseinate.
Albumen	White of egg, used to bind feed.
Trout pellets	Concentrated animal foodstuff.
Bovril	Beef extract.
Marmite	Yeast extract.
Complan	Invalid and baby food based on milk.
Wheat gluten	Used as a binding agent.
Soya flour	Provides bulk and high food value.
TVP	Textured vegetable protein.
Dried milk powder	Baby food.
Fish meal	Pure material for animal feed.
Corn meal	Animal feed and the bulk cereal behind breakfast foods.

Seed and corn baits

Wheat	Stewed when used as hookbait.
Hemp	Stewed when used as hookbait.
Tares	Wild pea seeds.
Sweetcorn	Undried maize: corn on the cob.
Beans	Butter and kidney, haricot, soya and broad beans can all be softened by steeving: possible carp baits.
Pearl barley	A stewed seed bait for river fish.
Potato	Par-boiled as a carp bait.
Peas	A soft bait but rarely used.

Bread baits

Crust	From the outer part of a fresh loaf.
Flake	The inner material from a new loaf.
Paste	Made from a semi-stale loaf.
Balanced crust	Paste pressed onto a crust to reduce the buoyancy.

Groundbait materials

Breadcrumb	Baked, ground and sieved crumbs.
Rusk	Cereal used in sausage manufacture.
Ground maize	An expensive bulk ingredient with an attractive colour when in the water.
Soil and mud	Used to give bulk and weight to groundbait mixtures.
Peat	Finely textured garden peat gives bulk and colour.
Silver sand	Varying the amount can create a cloud effect or make a fast-sinking attractor.

Groundbait additives: for taste

Cheese	Useful for chub and barbel.
Aniseed	An attractor for a wide variety of species.
Vanilla	Carp anglers used to use it a great deal (easily available as custard powder).
Sugar	Brown sugar is said to attract carp but also useful as a sticky, binding material.
Ground hemp	Produces oil which attracts many fish species.
Fish oil	Pilchard oil is most easily bought.
Hookbaits	Small pieces of worm, samples of maggots and tiny pieces of crust or flake.
Pigeon droppings	A Continental idea.
Arrowroot	An attractor with a binding property.

Fruits and berries

Elderberries	An autumn dapping bait.
Currants	An autumn dapping bait.
Apple, pear, banana	Possible change baits.

Crustaceans and molluscs

Crayfish	Gathered from clean, flowing streams —a chub bait.
Shrimps	Netted from the gravel of streams.
Swan mussels	A good tench bait netted from shallow, muddy water.
Snails	Both land and water snails have bait value.
Slugs	Make a good chub bait in the right hands.

Meat baits

Luncheon meat	Fished for chub and barbel as small cubes.
Sausage meat	Used as sausage meat or in skins.
Meat paste	Made from minced meat added to a cereal binder.

Cheese

Hard varieties	Fished as cubes on the hook.
Cheese paste	Made from the softer cheeses. Can be added to bread paste as taste attractor.

Fish baits

Herring	Pike deadbait.
Mackerel	Pike deadbait.
Sprats	Pike deadbait or as sink-and-draw baits.
Minnows	Fished as livebait or on a spinning flight.
Freshwater fish	As live or deadbaits for pike, perch and zander. Eels will also take deadbaits.

The Sea Fisher's Baits

Worms

Lugworms	Dug from a sand/mud mixture foreshore.
Ragworms	Found on muddy shores.
Catworm (white rag)	Found on muddy shores.

Shellfish

Razorfish	Found at the lowest spring tide mark.
Cockles	Rake them from under sand.
Clams	Dug from sand/mud beach.
Scallops	Trawled from sandy bottoms.
Mussels	Form colonies on piling, breakwaters and on rocks.
Welks	Trawled in deepish water.
Limpets	Gathered from lower rock shore.
Winkles	Gathered from lower rock shore.
Dog whelks	Found among acorn barnacles on the rocky shore and on the underside of stones.
Saddle oyster	Found at the lowest spring tide margin on a broken rock shore.
Piddock	Bores into lime and sandstone cliffs below the high tide mark.

Crustaceans

Prawns and shrimps	Found in rock pools and can be netted in shallow water on sandy beaches.
Shore crabs	Live among the weed and stones on the lower shore.

Fish bait

Mackerel	The best of sea angling baits (May–Nov).
Herring	Oily but soft bait for winter fishing.
Sandeels	Small sandeels can be scraped from a sandy beach at low tide. Larger sandeels are netted or feathered for.
Rockfish	Can be gathered from rockpools after a receding tide.
Sprats	A useful bait in winter and for sink-and-draw tactics with a preserved bait.
Pouting	A conger bait, dead.
Other species	A belly strip from most members of the cod family will be taken at times.

Odd Marine creatures

Squid and cuttlefish	Both members of the shellfish group (Mollusca) they make good baits fished whole or as strips.

Groundbait (rubby dubby)

Mashed mackerel	Can be used mixed together
Bran and sawdust	Preferably a little high.
Sand	As a carrier for the oil.
Pilchard oil	Gives weight to the oil and fish particles. An additive for taste and smell. Can also be used to give life to hookbaits.

INDEX

ACKNOWLEDGEMENTS

Chris Jones, for his tackle and technical illustrations.

Trevor King, of Dubery's Fishing Tackle, Hornchurch, Essex, for the bait preparation.

Mustad, of Norway, for the hook charts.

Len Cacutt, for copy editing and advice.

Robin L. K. Wood, for his publishing advice.

Goodwin Dorman, for their design.

Joyce West, for assistance in bait-digging.

Harold Prichard, the author's grandfather, who showed him how to couple a sporting life with humility.

Asjelien Baarslag, for the European aspect of the author's understanding of the sport of angling.

And all those anglers who have given freely of their experiences over many years of fishing and trauma.